Living the Story

Living the Story: The Ignatian Way of Prayer

Joseph Cassidy

Edited by Ann Loades

CANTERBURY
PRESS
Norwich

© The Estate of Joe Cassidy 2020

First published in 2020 by the Canterbury Press Norwich
Editorial office
3rd Floor, Invicta House
108–114 Golden Lane
London EC1Y 0TG, UK
www.canterburypress.co.uk

Canterbury Press is an imprint of Hymns Ancient & Modern Ltd
(a registered charity)

Hymns Ancient & Modern® is a registered trademark of
Hymns Ancient & Modern Ltd
13A Hellesdon Park Road, Norwich,
Norfolk NR6 5DR, UK

British Library Cataloguing in Publication data

A catalogue record for this book is available
from the British Library

978 1 78622 247 3

Typeset by Manila Typesetting Company
Printed and bound in Great Britain by
CPI Group (UK) Ltd

With thanks to Eileen and Lawrence Reynolds,
William Hyland and William Apedaile

For Gillian, Emmeline, Marianne and Benedict

Contents

Joseph Cassidy: Imagination, Scripture and Living a Christian Life

Joseph Patrick Michael Cassidy (JPC hereafter) was born in Canada in August 1954 into a family network of predominantly Irish and French origin. Baptized as a Roman Catholic, he became a Jesuit (a member of the Society of Jesus), was ordained as a priest, but for just over the last 20 years of his life became first a layman in the Church of England, then a priest in the Diocese of Salisbury. From 1997 to 2015 (the year in which he died) he was Principal of St Chad's College in the University of Durham. One of his projects was to offer to members of the Church of England – whether lay or ordained – his understanding of Ignatian spirituality. The contents of this present book integrate the drafts of his own contribution with that understanding together with some of his published work as an Anglican. The text also draws on his unpublished drafts and 'presentations' to a range of audiences, available to the editor of the material included here by courtesy of his widow, Dr Gillian Skinner.

Life and work

JPC grew up in Montreal, athletic, musical, with a marked talent for 'electronics' – in which he could have made his career – and excellent in his academic work. This latter characteristic was typical of him life-long. In his first year at Loyola College, Concordia University, Montreal (1972), he won the 'Match of the Minds' competition for full tuition, graduating as 'Loyola Scholar' at graduation in 1976. In a series of further degrees in both philosophy and theology he graduated with the highest distinction, culminating in his doctoral degree of 1995, awarded in 1996 by the University of Ottawa, and awarded the University's Gold Medal for the most outstanding doctoral thesis of the year. His degrees were gained as part and parcel of the vocation he found first as a member of the Society of Jesus, and then beyond it, integrating 'academic' work with 'spirituality' and exercising marked abilities both as teacher and administrator.

JPC's sense of vocation developed from some profoundly important life-changing experiences, which he recalled both to himself and for others on a number of occasions, the first of which especially became a kind of 'touchstone' for him whenever he had to make a major decision in the course of his life. Early in his university career, half-in and half-out of sleep one night, he came to the realization that 'if it were true that God existed, and if it were true that God became a human being, and if you really did believe such an unbelievable thing, then that had to be the most important thing in your life: what dignity, what an incredibly powerful thing to do, so unlikely, and yet so wonderful at the same time.' Shortly afterwards, he happened to meet up with his College Chaplain who invited him for a chat, and on hearing JPC's account of his reflections, opened his Bible at Philippians 2, and read there the 'poem of invitation' to 'put on the mind of Christ'. Life-long, JPC retained a sense of 'the utter glory' and 'the infinite generosity of God', having glimpsed 'infinite divine Trinitarian self-emptying'. He took every opportunity to preach and teach with confidence Trinitarian faith, the heart of which is that 'ultimate reality is Trinitarian, relational and communal' (see Spirituality and the Trinity below).

He was to write:

My original experience taught me that God is found in self-sacrificing love. If you want to see God, if you want to see what infinite love looks like, if you want to see the power of God, you have to look to Jesus, his life and his preaching, to his cross. If you want to see the divinity of Jesus, you have to look to his self-emptying, for it is in that self-emptying, that humility, which is the very humility of God, that we encounter God face-to-face, that we taste something of the glory of God. For me, that encounter with the self-emptying Jesus is my way into the mystery of God, it is how God chooses to encounter me, it is how God calls me back to him, whenever I get too far away. What is your experience? How has God called you? How does God choose to encounter you?

Between school and university in 1972 he undertook three months of general military training, and then worked as a volunteer at a hostel for homeless people. The following year he joined the Society of Jesus, that is, becoming a 'companion' or 'comrade' of Jesus, his radical response to the 'poem of invitation' he continued to hear. Professed in 1979, he was committed to possibly a 13-year-long process of prayer, study and placements as a layman, before consideration of ordination as a priest. Study and some demanding placements apart, the core necessity was rigorous engagement with the 'Spiritual Exercises' – workouts devised by St Ignatius Loyola (see below), the goal being 'in contemplation to attain love' (see the hymn 'My God, I love thee' by St Francis Xavier, number 524 in *Common Praise*, Canterbury Press, 2000). Almost entirely based on the gospels, the intention was and remains to become free enough to follow the divine will, supported by a 'director', learning discernment and freedom from self-deception. JPC himself became a valued director and teacher both of Scripture and Spirituality, for both lay and ordained, not least in the life-long attention he gave to his sermons.

Experience as a Pastoral Assistant in Jamaica and then, at his own request, in Nicaragua as the 'contra' war was breaking out, precipitated him into exploring a vocation to the priesthood (ordained deacon in 1985, and to the priesthood in 1986), and whole-hearted commitment in both organizations to what would now be identified as 'political theology', and publications focused on Latin America. His motivation was clear: 'There is urgent work to be done. There are all too many people in our world with footprints on their back', suffering because of our sins, greed, paralysis, in which we need to rise to the challenges both of rewarding hard work and initiative in making the world work better; sharing success, but also attending to those unfortunate at home as well as in places of exceptional difficulty such as Central America. He knew perfectly well how both social and economic structures put relationships in jeopardy at the most fundamental levels of society, and was unequivocally committed to arguing that human beings have 'a daunting responsibility creatively to construct the good'. He developed skills as a broadcaster as well as a writer both in Canada and eventually on BBC Radio Solent in the UK, thereby engaging with many people well outside ecclesial structures.

Once ordained, JPC had another profoundly important experience, connected to his father's dying, which resulted in his own life taking a different turn from what he had so far expected. For as his father lay dying, and seeing his children one by one, JPC saw his father reaching up to touch his mother's cheek, a tenderness JPC immediately realized he would never know in his life as a celibate. Furthermore, his father said to him that he would not be disappointed were JPC both to leave the Jesuits and to marry. 'He knew me better than I knew myself.' Never regretting his life as a celibate, in which he had discovered a desire for communion with God and established his prayer life, nonetheless JPC did indeed leave the Society of Jesus in 1991, and after a stint as a Diocesan priest in Toronto, in 1992 successfully applied for the post of Senior Lecturer in Ethics and Spirituality at the College of La Sainte Union (LSU), then one of a group of colleges (including two Church of England theological colleges and a Roman Catholic Seminary) under the aegis of the University of Southampton. LSU was focused on teacher-training, but also offered a degree in Philosophy and Theology. Short of a Chaplain, JPC agreed to undertake this responsibility for a year, having made it clear that he might be leaving the priesthood. At LSU he re-thought his teaching material for his new context, began to publish his work again, not least in economics and social theory. He also studied an extraordinary range of topics of immediate importance as these presented themselves to the general public. At the same time he worked at what turned out to be an outstandingly good doctorate, presented in 1995 and awarded in 1996. He also set up the LSU Centre for Ignatian Lay Spirituality, to be affiliated to other centres in the UK, the USA and Rome. Marrying Gillian (a specialist in English Literature on the staff of LSU) concluded his time as a priest in the Roman Catholic Church. After returning to the laity he was to find another ordained vocation in the Church of England, becoming a Non-Stipendiary Minister and an assistant curate in two parishes in the Diocese of Salisbury. He had always been acutely aware that ordination was the effect of the prayers of others for him, to enter into a web of relationships with them, inter-dependent with them on God. He realized yet again that priesthood was to be focused on the radicalism of 'actually living the gospel with humility and honesty and integrity and passion, and, perhaps most importantly, with others'.

Existing publications apart, the completion of his doctorate would have been important for his career development even if LSU had survived beyond 1997 (the year of its closure), but it happened to be a key element in his success in being appointed Principal of St Chad's College, University of Durham, an Anglican foundation much in need of someone who could re-establish the College in the tradition of some of its distinguished Principals. To take the doctorate first: *Extending Bernard Lonergan's Ethics* introduced to Durham the work of a most formidable member of the Society of Jesus, relatively little known in the UK, notwithstanding some 29 volumes of his published work, and 19 honorary doctorates. JPC hoped to establish a British Lonergan Association and had plans – if and when time permitted – to publish parts of his thesis, and possibly the whole of it suitably revised, a familiar task for anyone completing a doctorate. His appreciation of Lonergan's importance for the understanding of the interplay between imagination, spirituality and ethics was explained in the Introduction to Lonergan's work that he published in the journal *Foundation*, published annually by St Chad's, and it became familiar to those he encountered in the many lectures and retreats with which he was concerned up and down the Church of England. He urged his hearers to be attentive, intelligent, reasonable and responsible, to discover the links between their feelings, appetites, needs, desires, hopes, commitments. The dream he commended was that of 'an integrated life, where every bit of our lives, every decision we make, is suffused by grace, directed by grace, and fulfilled in grace' (the last chapter of his thesis was focused on 'The above downwards dynamic of grace'). He began to explore and integrate his experience of imagination in prayer and discernment of appropriate action with Trinitarian theology, sacraments and ethics and the generous practice of authority and ecumenism within and beyond the Church of England.

So far as the College of St Chad was concerned, it was entirely appropriate that its members learned of JPC's perspectives in chapel, but also in his establishment of a full-time team of research staff, a variety of Fellowships and the practice of 'discernment' within the College's structures, sorting out buildings, finances, governance and management, recruitment of both under- and post-graduate students and the priority to be given to the establishment of an academic ethos comparable in new circumstances to that in which he himself had flourished. Ignatian spirituality and the capacity to imagine times, places and people anew now cohered with a Jesuit tradition from the earliest years of the Society: that of taking seriously the conduct of educational institutions, of vital importance to his College. Above all, the spiritual freedom he had discovered in the Ignatian tradition he wanted to commend to whoever would attend to what he had to offer his hearers and readers, not least the laity in the endless variety of their commitments. Hence this book, so far as possible put together from JPC's own drafts for it, and from his other writing whether published or not.

An Introduction to Ignatian Prayer

Background: Ignatius and the Spiritual Exercises

Ignatian prayer grew out of the experience of St Ignatius of Loyola, the founder of the Jesuits (1491–1556). Injured as a young man and confined to bed, he slipped back and forth between his awareness of his hospital surroundings and the chivalrous dreams of a young Basque. As might happen to anyone in similar circumstances, Ignatius couldn't help but ask the tougher questions concerning his life; and these questions led to his strong convictions about the vanities of his times. He became enamoured of the example of saints such as Benedict and Francis of Assisi. He read accounts of their lives, the rules for their communities, as well as books on the lives of other saints. He saw no reason why he, too, couldn't do something radical and all-consuming for the Lord; so he took his cue from his newfound heroes and decided to pattern his life on the imitation of Jesus Christ.

For Ignatius, this imitation of Christ would be as literal as possible; and after much searching and hopeless attempts at self-denial, he and his companions set off on a pilgrimage to the Holy Land. They had dreamt of founding a small community, much like the Franciscans who were in charge of many of the holy places. Ignatius committed himself to one condition as he went forward: he would defer to the Pope by letting the Pope decide whether they should remain in the Holy Land. This deference was to play an important role when he eventually founded the Jesuit order, but initially it pointed to a healthy respect on Ignatius' part for the possibility that he might be doing his own will and not God's. Their plan came to naught, an eventuality which they had foreseen, as their plan to settle down was thwarted by the administrator of the Holy Land.

Despite the collapse of that initial dream, the underlying desire to imitate Christ persisted. Though he remained passionately committed to finding Christ, Ignatius no longer thought that following Christ meant tracing the geographical pattern of his life. Instead he began to see more and more clearly that this following of Christ would be a clinging to the strategy and person of Christ in the decisions of our daily lives – both the large vocational decisions, as well as the seemingly mundane.

Today, as then, this doing of God's will depends on finding or 'discerning' God's will. It means getting to know Jesus, who was *the* clearest expression of what following God's will means and entails. Needless to say, this familiarity with Jesus does not occur overnight; it really is a journey in faith which covers the spans of all our lives.

The Spiritual Exercises of St Ignatius is a small book of instructions for retreat directors, which outlines a suggested procedure for entering into this journey of faith. Most of the suggested prayer material is based on the Gospels themselves; and Ignatius suggests that we try to enter into the gospel stories by using our imaginations to make the story come alive. Quite deliberately, the person making the Exercises is led through the life of Christ as it is depicted in the Gospels, beginning with the Incarnation and ending – not simply with the Resurrection – but with Christ's enduring presence throughout all of creation.

The goal of the Exercises is a 'putting on the mind and heart of Jesus' – a grace prayed for, not in these exact words, but in

2

numerous other ways. The person making the Exercises prays for an intense love of Jesus and an uncompromising desire to follow him. Perhaps most profoundly of all, this grace is experienced as a spiritual freedom, the willingness to follow Jesus no matter the cost. This grace is received when it begins to spill over into our whole lives. Ignatius hoped that those who made the Exercises would reach a level of freedom which would allow them to make all of their human decisions based solely on whatever helped them most to praise, love, and serve God.

The type of Ignatian prayer espoused here attempts to integrate some of the key insights of the Exercises with a form of prayer based on the person of Jesus. The beauty of praying on the person of Jesus through the Gospels is its simplicity. It doesn't require years of spiritual training beyond the reach of any well-meaning Christian. It doesn't require mastery of weird or esoteric techniques. Fortunately enough, it requires only a heartfelt desire to know and love Jesus and a facility for day-dreaming. Though we may not admit it readily, most of us are well-practised at day-dreaming.

Why the Gospels?

There is something to be said for praying on a single gospel for an extended period of time. It is one of the most effective ways of appreciating a particular gospel-writer's unique perspective on Jesus. Each gospel-writer (or 'evangelist') tells us everything he thinks we need to know to fall in love with Jesus and to follow him.

Our lives as Christians have everything to do with a conversion to discipleship, an actual turning and following Jesus of Nazareth. But we can't follow nothing; discipleship cannot occur in a vacuum; so we require some knowledge of how Jesus actually lived; how he made decisions, his priorities, his activities, his commitments. Our following Jesus has to be concrete, has to affect our real life, day-to-day decisions, or we are, in effect, saying that Jesus is largely irrelevant to our lives.

The possibility of our following Jesus today depends also on our recognizing that the Risen Lord *is* the historical Jesus. That is to say, the same Jesus who walked in Palestine calls us to discipleship today. One of the beauties of our faith is that the person we read about in the Gospels is still a human being; he still has a personality and emotions; he can remember all the events written about him. Presumably, he is able to look back in fondness, recalling how his apostles messed up; he remembers what it feels like to be rejected; he remains able to feel compassion for the poor and downtrodden. The good news of the Resurrection is that Jesus, the Jesus his disciples knew and loved, *that* Jesus was raised up and is alive today. That same Jesus calls us to follow in his footsteps.

The Gospels differ from each other because they really do tell different stories – different conversion stories, different appreciations of what was important, different ideas about how best to tell THE story. Just as we might want to ask a number of people about someone or something to get as many points of view as possible, the gospel-writers present us with a rich and necessary diversity. No one person could fully appreciate all that Jesus said, taught, and did. No one person fully appreciated the meaning of that life. But the Gospels do contain the memories and experiences of those who knew Jesus best; and each gospel reveals a true and crucial side of Jesus' life and personality.

Because each evangelist had his own privileged point of view, some people find it helpful to pray through a particular gospel from start to finish, using a different gospel passage for each prayer period (or even repeating the same one a number of times). It is a fair assumption that each evangelist had his own reasons for ordering things the way he did. It's as though each had said to us that we had to understand this particular teaching of Jesus before we could understand a particular action. This suggested approach may help to ensure that we don't get an image of Jesus made of 'snapshots' of him from all over the place. Instead we can slowly develop a well-rounded idea of what he was like from each of the evangelists, one by one.

Another advantage of sticking to one gospel and to that gospel's own ordering of materials is the possibility of our letting Scripture set our prayer agenda. Though not everyone would agree on this, I like to let the life of Jesus, through particular gospel passages, lead me – rather than always praying on what *I* might want to pray about. This way, I can let the life, the teachings, the strategies of Jesus challenge me. I let the life of Jesus assert my life's agenda. Of course, this can't be considered an absolute rule, for there are plenty of times when I really should be praying on what presently concerns me most: to do otherwise might be to deceive myself; and it might even represent a lack of faith on my part, somehow thinking that, unless I pray on the 'right' material, the Lord will be unable to break through to me.

So let me suggest a Method of Prayer.

Pick a passage

An important step in Ignatian prayer is to pick a gospel and a gospel passage. Often people find it helpful to start with the particular gospel of the Church Cycle, and even to start with the gospel text which corresponds to the current season of the Church's calendar. Whatever you choose, look over it before you begin your prayer. Get a quick feel for what's in the passage.

Where do I pray?

Jesus seemed to prefer quiet, lonely places; I often prefer the same, but it's important that each person find his or her own special place. I usually take a few moments and consider what sort of mood I'm in, how susceptible I am to distractions; and then I choose a spot accordingly. Perhaps I'm tired and I need the reminders of a chapel or a church to keep me focused. Perhaps I'm feeling a bit down and burdened and would prefer a place where I might be able to sob or sigh without distracting others.

When do I pray?

I don't have a lot of hard evidence for this, but I can't help but feel that Jesus had a hard time 'getting his prayer in' – in much the same way that many of us find it hard to take time to pray. Jesus found it so difficult to be 'regular' in prayer, that he had to steal away from crowds, he had to spend whole nights in prayer. I often wonder whether those long nights were his way of making up for lost time!

When we get down to it, prayer is important to us, not because we are under an obligation to pray, but because it was so evidently important in Jesus' life. For instance, it is not inconsequential for us that Jesus experienced God's approval of him when he was in prayer after his baptism. Nor is it beside the point to notice that it was after the desert, after a prolonged period of prayer and fasting, that Jesus undertakes his whole mission, presumably in response to whatever happened during his prayer in the desert. Again, the other powerful experience of God's approval of Jesus occurred also during prayer at the Transfiguration.

So when should we pray? Looking to Luke's gospel, we see that Jesus prayed before leaving places (Luke 4.42); when he was tired (Luke 5.16); before making big decisions like choosing the apostles (Luke 6.12); before and during the Transfiguration (Luke 9.28); when he was happy (Luke 10.21); when he had something on his mind (Luke 21.37); when he was alone in the garden in Jerusalem 'as was his custom' (Luke 22.38); when he was in agony (Luke 22.42; 23.34; 23.46) and of course, when he was on the cross. If we are to follow Jesus as fellow prayers, we, like Jesus, will spend some quality time by ourselves or whenever we are conscious of something good or bad, important, sad, unusual happening in our lives. Like Jesus, we'll go to prayer when we are discouraged or overjoyed, puzzled or very sure of ourselves, tired or full of strength.

What time of day? Who knows? Some people pray better in the morning when they're wide awake; others, like Jesus perhaps, prayed when they could, and that's often easiest late at night when there's nothing else to do, or when sleeping is difficult because they've got something on their minds.

How often? Some people pray every day. Some people think everyone should pray every day. Some people are obviously different from me; more disciplined, more able to make decisions and stick to them. One thing for sure, if you're not the type to keep to a schedule, go easy on yourself. The following pattern is not all that unusual:

- I start off saying I'll pray every day.
- I start off well for the first few weeks.
- I miss a few days.
- I feel guilty.
- I miss a few more days because I feel guilty.
- I can't remember when I prayed last.

Rather than say that you're going to pray every day, and then miss a few days, why not aim for something realistic? Say you'll pray three or four times a week. And if you find you're just not making it, change your plans to something more realistic. Maybe you'll end up deciding that you can only pray during marathon prayer periods, and you decide to take a morning or evening every week or two.

One thing that many people find helpful, however, is setting a time-limit for each prayer period and sticking to it. So, if I decide that I'm going to pray for a half hour, I commit myself to listening to God for a half-hour, no matter if the prayer seems to be the worst of my life or the screaming best. The Lord knows quite well how much time I've got, how much time I've set aside, and the Lord who invented time is also quite effective in working within time-limits.

What do I do with my body?

Postures can be prayers – non-vocal prayers which use our entire bodies. Ignatius suggests that we begin with an initial profound act or gesture of reverence to facilitate our entry into prayer. Sometimes I conjure up some posture which expresses what I actually feel towards the Lord. For instance, if I'm feeling distant from God, I sometimes bunch myself up in a corner to pray; but when I'm feeling particularly joyful, I'll sometimes pray on my back with my arms extended. To be honest, I love praying in the bathtub – and I'm not really sure what that means!

'When I'm comfortable I fall asleep: and when I'm uncomfortable I can't pray'. If this sounds familiar, you may just be praying at the wrong time, or you may need to try a style of prayer which engages your mind a bit more. You might want to take a stab at praying outside, walking around. Whatever you choose, don't get in a position so uncomfortable that your body becomes the focus of your prayer instead of the Lord.

Then what?

After I've got my passage, and I'm in the right place and in the right position, I use a little prayer to help quiet myself down, a sort of focusing. I give myself some time (3 to 5 minutes) to let the desires of Jesus' Spirit, which have been planted deep within me, rise to consciousness. The precise words aren't all that important, but the desires are crucial.

> I beg the Lord to attract me so that all my intentions, actions, desires, dreams and inclinations, my whole life and being will be focused on God. My only reason for asking is that I might praise, love and serve my God for ever.

What I'm probing for is some sort of resonance of this prayer, this desire, with my whole being. If it really doesn't seem to be an honest desire on my part, I place myself humbly in God's hands and admit that my desire and faith are weak. I ask God to draw me closer, to reveal to me that somehow my deepest desires will be fulfilled in God alone.

After this very quiet, relaxed, 'getting in touch with myself and God' prayer, I usually need to remind myself that I'm not praying alone, and so I quite consciously call upon the Holy Spirit. Though this isn't explicitly in the Exercises, it can be a very helpful step for many people, because it sums up what we really desire, what we really believe in. The unfortunate thing is that this 'praying for the Spirit' often gets complicated because we've tended to make a mess of the Holy Spirit: it's not news that many of us aren't quite sure what we're praying for when we do invoke the Holy Spirit.

We need to recall that even though Scripture speaks of the Spirit in a number of different ways, one tradition suggests that Jesus promised his very own Spirit to us, the Spirit that he shared with his Father. However we understand the Spirit, it is not an anonymous or faceless spirit. No, it is the very depths of Jesus, himself – whatever it was that made him 'tick'. It is the deepest source of Jesus' strength: his hope, his trust, his undying faith in his Father. It is the living Spirit behind the words of his teachings, the spirit of the beautiful dream which fuelled his teachings, his commitment to the Kingdom of God. It is whatever made him capable of acting as though God really reigned on this earth and that nothing else actually mattered. Happily, it is the same Spirit that was given to us in baptism, the very Spirit of Jesus, the Spirit that Jesus and his Father share. Nothing less. He promised us *his* very own Spirit.

When we say we want to put on the mind and heart of Jesus, we can fall into a 'distant' form of mimicry. But when we admit that putting on the mind and heart of Jesus requires that we be united to him at the very core of our beings, then this praying for the Spirit makes sense. We acknowledge that we believe in Jesus' promise by invoking the Spirit in prayer, and we really do live out of our faith when we actually wait a few moments for the Spirit to well up tangibly within us. And so it's important not simply to pray for this Spirit but actually to *receive* the Spirit, actually to *wait* a few minutes for the Spirit's presence to register with our minds and hearts.

After a few minutes, I'm ready to focus even more precisely on what I want. In some way or another, verbally or not, I pray that I might truly encounter Jesus, so that I might put on his mind and heart. I pray that my entire life will be shaped by him, that I might love him and follow him ever more closely.

Just to review for a moment, I find it helpful to prepare my prayer ahead of time, and to begin leisurely. Though I'm inconsistent, somehow my prayer involves the following ingredients: choosing a passage and reading it once, making an act of reverence, focusing on God and invoking the Spirit, and begging to be able to know and follow Jesus.

The most important thing, of course, is to forget these 'steps' immediately. If we want to find a way of praying which offers us any likelihood that our prayer might become a significant part of our lives, then it is critical that each of us find his or her own way of preparing for, and entering into prayer: patiently, authentically, peacefully, reverently, expectantly.

The Gospel passage

After I am conscious of being in the Lord's presence, I then read through the gospel passage once without pausing, getting familiar with the whole scene. I may reread it again if I'm not getting an impression of the event or scene.

I then read the same passage again, but slowly this time. I notice any details which strike me, anything which puzzles or intrigues me, anything which causes any reaction at all in me.

Then I close the Scriptures and either:

a) *Imagine* the scene occurring with me as a participant or an involved observer. I use each of my five senses to be present. I might remind myself that I am participating in the Lord's memory of the event, and I try to enter into his memory, to share it anew. Throughout, I try to keep focused on Jesus, to interact with him and the other gospel personalities.

Or

b) *Consider* how Jesus is being revealed, what he is saying about himself, what I can learn of his personality, his attitudes, his desires. I try to get inside the person of Jesus; and *I avoid moralizing or looking for a message.* The important thing is to remain focused on Jesus.

The warning to avoid moralizing is underlined because it's a great temptation for those beginning in prayer. Many of us were taught to read the Gospels as if they were something like Aesop's fables: each one has a little moral message for boys and girls. The saddest part of that type of early training is that many of us never quite get over it. We fail to realize that when we moralize the Gospels, we are taking our eyes off Jesus; we are reducing the life of Jesus to the types of characters Aesop wrote about.

Perhaps some examples may help. Imagine someone praying on Jesus' washing of the disciples' feet. Some people will immediately start looking for the 'personal message' Jesus has for them in this story; and they'll conclude something like 'Jesus wants me to be nice to people'. Well, aside from the egoism involved here, Jesus probably wouldn't have any little 'message' for them anyway. After all, there's no great need for a new message: the message has already been given. Nothing is hidden. The message is Jesus' whole life, how he got to this point, why he thought this was a fitting last 'teaching'. The goal is not simply to say, 'Oh, that was nice of Jesus'. No, much more than that, the goal is to let Jesus' humility, his non-violent, non-coercive way of leadership, his truly affectionate love of his disciples – to let all this and more both delight my heart and, at the same time challenge my every desire and notion of what it means to follow Jesus. When we start moralizing or looking for messages, we've already taken our eyes off Jesus and placed them squarely on ourselves.

Abide with me

I usually try to spend some time each prayer period either chatting with the Lord, or remaining profoundly silent in his presence. I try to let the encounter run deeper; I try to let the Lord tug at the core of my being, let him entice me at my deepest levels. I luxuriate in his presence, or, if he seems absent, I wait quietly, faced with my own profound emptiness. I wait in adoration, knowing that at this moment, I can do nothing other than wait, that I am not God, that I am God's creature.

The key to wasting time is realizing that it is *our time*, God's and my time, to do or say or be with each other; and it doesn't matter terribly how we spend the time.

So you try not to moralize. So you avoid looking for messages. But, then nothing happens! Don't worry. You can't pray incorrectly. A powerful experience of the Lord's presence is not a reward for praying successfully or correctly. The real art of prayer is learning how to 'dispose ourselves', how to desire the Lord and yet confess that we are entirely dependent on the Lord. Prayer methods are ways people have found to stay focused – if only for a second at a time – on the Lord. We cannot make it happen.

It's important to remember that prayer methods have no value in themselves: they're not tricks, nor secret recipes for communicating with God. They're certainly not sacraments. No, they are simply the fruits of centuries of Christian prayer. Rather than esoteric techniques guaranteed to work, prayer methods offer us the possibility of *not* worrying so much about the mechanics of prayer, *not* trying to *solve* prayer, *not* trying to unlock the secret formulae of successful prayer. Prayer methods are a means of getting my attention off myself and what I'm doing; they're habits of listening, preventative medicine for those among us who would 'junk up' their prayer.

So when nothing seems to be happening, we trust. In faith, we know that God desires to reveal himself to us. God desires that we know of his presence, that we learn to trust in his love. As we said, there are no secrets. Jesus is the sufficient and complete revelation of God. There isn't anything very important that he forgot to tell us, anything absolutely crucial that the gospel-writers neglected to include. When nothing seems to be happening, it's not because we haven't found 'the secret' yet.

Coping with dryness

There are a number of reasons for the feeling that nothing's happening in prayer. It's called 'dryness' by those who know, only too well, just what that experience is all about. Over the years, people who pray have come to understand that the Lord might have something in mind when we are allowed to experience dryness. Here are a few of the reasons:

- Sometimes we begin to think that we are in control of the prayer, that *we've* found *the* technique. At some point, the Lord will remind us that this is simply not the case.
- Often the Lord seems to invite us to let go of, say, a childish image of God; and he, by letting us experience distance from him, teaches us that he's not really who we thought he was. For instance, I might have the notion that the Lord is pulling strings, making everything work to my advantage. Well, the Lord might just decide that we're ready for the more adult notion that God is not 'the Great Protector in the sky'. We can expect to be taught that the disciples of Jesus follow Jesus at some real costs. The Lord may simply not 'be there' when we approach him in this way. It's as though we had dialled up the 'Great Protector' and find out that there never really was anyone at that number.

- Often enough, we can get 'hooked' on the delight which comes from being closer to God. We can become more concerned about the good feelings than about God. The solution? God pulls back just enough that we no longer experience delight or closeness. We are thus invited to love God for God's sake alone, but in the process we feel abandoned.

- At other times our decisions may have taken us away from God, we may have opted for a different set of values to Jesus'; we may have chosen something which gives us power, wealth, or prestige. God will try to let us know that such decisions really do make a difference; they really do pull us away from God; they really do constitute our departing from Jesus' path and strategy. God will let us know that the path leads to nowhere, or worse. Again, dryness may result until I wake up and realize what I'm doing to myself.

- Dryness may be as simple a phenomenon as an invitation to look for God at a deeper or more mature level of my being. It can be likened to a mother letting go of a child so that the child can learn how to walk; the mother, of course, knows that the child will never learn unless she puts the child down. She actually has to let the child go – even though the child will feel abandonment and fear.

- Some of us *need* to experience dryness if we are that type of person who wants God to 'draw' them, to 'attract' them in such a way that an adult choice of concretely walking with Jesus day-to-day wouldn't be necessary. This can be subtle and can last for years. If I am asking God to possess me, God will have little choice but to withdraw.

- Others have such an unrealistic and inhuman picture of Jesus that the prayer can never pass 'the reality test'. Their prayer is 'cute'; they have no real appreciation of Jesus' struggles and hard decisions; they, for whatever reasons, avoid pain, avoid reality, and live in a fantasy world. Though I am sure that the

Lord will never cease to bend over backwards trying to get through to such people, still he wouldn't reinforce those sorts of attitudes. The Lord will simply not be a party to falsehood. The Lord's absence will be experienced as dryness.

- The Lord sometimes does remove himself (though not completely, otherwise we would cease to exist) to let us know just how present he normally is. We can take him for granted so easily.

- Sometimes we can even pray for dryness without realizing it. For instance, I may be praying to experience myself as loveable in and of myself with no reference to God's loving me. So the Lord pulls back and lets me experience my loveableness without him. Or I might be praying that I might not be so needy, that I be more independent, and the Lord answers that prayer by stepping back. It might only be then that I realize something's wrong.

- Perhaps most importantly, we ought to remember that the experience of dryness is simply a part of Christian life. We are a 'waiting' people. Perfect union with God remains something we hope for, something we quite literally, at times, groan for. At various points in our lives, we will feel this 'groaning' most profoundly and painfully; and it will seem like an emptiness, a lack, an insatiable hunger.

Quite frankly, I often have to stop and recall that Jesus must have experienced dryness in prayer; so from time to time, I try imagining myself sitting beside Jesus, and I imagine us both experiencing dryness or even aversion to prayer. If my imagination and desires seem completely shut down, then I don't try to do something foreign to me. I enter prayer and I admit that I'm really disgusted, turned-off, lonely, frustrated, angry, depressed – whatever; and I place myself in Jesus' presence no matter which passage I have chosen, and I imagine myself blind, dumb, feelingless, unresponsive – but all of these things at the Lord's side.

For example, if I can't imagine anything visually, I might just imagine myself as a blind person in a particular episode of Jesus' life. And if, in addition to being unable to see anything, I am unable even to hear Jesus or anyone else, then I'll imagine that I'm also deaf, and I'll simply try to 'sense' Jesus' presence in some other way.

Distractions

Often we 'suffer' from what people call 'distractions' in prayer. Everyone knows the experience of trying to pray when something seems to keep getting in the way: some thought, temptation, image, or concern seems to prevent us from focusing on the Lord. The first thing to realize is that sometimes this is simply something to take in our stride. There will be days when we will simply not be able to pray very much. We ought to consider making use of oral prayer, the rosary, or Scripture. Or, we can even just face the fact that this particular day is plainly not our day.

At other times, we will really want to pray, and we will try to face the distractions head on. If that's the case, an important principle is that distractions need be distractions only if we let them be distractions. A time-honoured, Jesuit way to deal with distractions is to include them right in your prayer. For instance, if you're a student and you can't get that paper you're supposed to write out of your mind, then be distracted with the Lord: picture yourself at the Sermon on the Mount, for instance, and imagine (since it's true) sitting there thinking about your paper instead of listening to Jesus. Or if you're worrying about making supper, say, while trying to pray on the Crucifixion, well, imagine yourself present at Calvary and let yourself day-dream about supper. You can even bring a microwave and an extension cord and make the supper right there next to Jesus. This may all seem absurd to you, but all you're doing is using your imagination to express what you truly feel: in fact, you want to focus on Jesus, but you're caught up with cooking. The worst thing you can do is to *pretend* that you are not worried about cooking when you really are. You are preoccupied, so admit it; use your imagination to make your conflicting desires come alive. That way, the Lord can address them.

The rule, if we can call it that, is to make sure that you are yourself in prayer, that you bring your real concerns into the prayer, that you don't try to 'censor' or control your prayer. People who pray regularly will tell you that it was often *because* they let distraction into their prayer that the Lord was able to break through. The student, for instance, may find that Jesus pauses in the middle of the Sermon on the Mount, and comes over and helps the student with her paper. The student feels that Jesus is really concerned about how she's doing, what she's studying. The student may discover that Jesus can imagine all kinds of ways in which her learning can help him bring about his dream of the Kingdom. Of course, it's *her* imagination, and yet there's something profoundly true about what she's imagining. The person cooking may find out that Jesus remained concerned about the practical things of life even when he was dying: the person praying might for the first time in his or her life realize the significance of Jesus asking John to care for his mother – the ability Jesus had even in death not to be entirely caught up in himself.

Just one other little point about distractions, especially distractions that seem to be temptations. They really do keep us humble; they keep our need for salvation ever before us. Sometimes we simply have to laugh at ourselves: here I am, all set for a great hour of prayer, and I just can't get my mind off 'x'. Rather than feel like a crumb, it's often a good time to accept God's invitation to be a part of the human race.

After it's over

Ignatius was insistent that we include a review of our prayer so that we can be more focused on the Lord during the actual prayer. So, after I finish praying, I get up and get a coffee or go for a walk. I look back over the prayer and ask what moved me. Did I feel attracted by the Lord? By someone or something else? Did I feel any aversion to anything in the prayer? Any road-blocks? Did I feel peaceful, afraid, tense, anxious, happy, sad, courageous, humbled, small, big, strong, weak, blessed, sinful, forgiven, loving, protected, vulnerable, tempted, hopeful? I consider what is behind my feelings.

I consider my distractions. Were they really distractions or was the Lord trying to say something to me? I ask myself whether I can detect any changes among how I felt upon entering into the prayer, how I felt throughout the prayer, and how I felt as I ended the prayer.

Did I notice anything about the Lord that I had never noticed before? Do I know him better today than yesterday? Do I desire to follow him more? Did I feel his personal presence or was I distant from him? Did he notice me in the prayer?

The list goes on, but the goal is the same: to try to get underneath the 'raw' experience of prayer to focus on the Lord. The reason for all of this is that it helps us develop a sense of where the Lord might be leading us, what the Lord might be trying to say to us.

The prayer review is an important tool to use when we are deciding on what to use for the next prayer time. St Ignatius has a bit of a rule which can help us: if I experience any significant attractions or aversions in my prayer (what he calls 'movements of consolation and desolation') then I return to them in my next prayer. In fact, I keep on returning to them until I have a fairly good sense that it's time to move on. If I change the focus of my prayer before then, it's as though I were telling the Lord, 'Lord, thanks for getting through to me, but I've really got to be moving on.'

A gentle nudge . . .

If you haven't got one already, once you get to the point of regularly having to decide (discern) what to pray on, whether to repeat a particular passage, and so on, you might think seriously about finding someone to speak with about your prayer, either a prayer companion or spiritual director.

Summary of the steps

- I choose a passage and read it once.
- I focus on the Lord and invoke the Holy Spirit of Jesus.
- I ask for what I want: to know and follow Jesus.
- I read the passage several times, then I either imagine or consider Jesus and the scene.
- I spend some quiet time with the Lord.
- I close my prayer with gratitude; and after my prayer is over, I do a review of my prayer.

An Introduction to Ignatian Prayer, Montreal: Ignatian Publications, 1988, was reprinted as *Praying the Gospels. An Introduction to Discipleship,* Montreal: Ignatian Spirituality Centre, 2003.

2

Further Reflections on
Ignatian Spirituality

Ignatian spirituality is not just for Jesuits! Long before any Jesuits existed, Ignatius was having spiritual conversations with people and leading them through the Spiritual Exercises – a prayerful journey through the life of Christ which, in some ways, paralleled Ignatius' own spiritual journey.

The heart of Ignatian spirituality is the quest for familiarity or intimacy with God. Such intimacy was not a flight back to the womb, but the kind of intimacy that allows two minds, two hearts, to beat as one. Ignatius was convinced that we could actually get a feel for God's preferences, that we could pattern our love on divine love, and in that way discover and very deliberately do God's will.

Ignatius sincerely believed that God worked hard to express divine love for us every minute of every day, and that our task is first to learn to recognize that love. In fact, Ignatius would have us become so attuned to God's presence, that we can notice when our impending decisions take us closer to or further away from God.

Learning to be attuned to God's presence does not come easily for most of us. To be sensitive to God's often gentle presence, to be able to notice when our preferences are in even the slightest tension with God's preferences – these require spiritual maturity and freedom.

None of this sounds very revolutionary, and yet adopting an Ignatian viewpoint can bring a wonderful sense of newness to life. Ignatian spirituality makes a huge claim: that I can, in particular decisions, discover what God actually wills me to do. This holds not only for individuals, but for groups, indeed for our whole planet. God has a divine strategy (though arguably not a preordained blueprint) and that strategy is to engage fully in a divine–human partnership to bring about God's dream for our future.

It is largely for this reason that Ignatian spirituality is so powerful. Ignatian spirituality challenges us to tune in to the rhythms of divine activity in our universe, to believe that God is personally involved in our world not just as a passive companion or behind-the-scenes facilitator, but as someone who is working through and on behalf of creation to bring it to a splendid completion. God chooses to involve us; God, in some senses, chooses to need us to complete the divine work; God chose to become one of us, in part to drive home the fact of just how complete and personal is the divine involvement in our world.

It would be a mistake to think of Ignatian spirituality as solely an approach to decision-making. Perhaps like all spirituality, Ignatian spirituality is a lifestyle: an integrated approach to life overall. Though there is a sense in which it is a school of spirituality, there is a larger sense in which Ignatian spirituality has to be so internalized as to constitute one's spontaneous world view. Ignatius' hope for Jesuits was that they would simply become familiar with God – a gentle hope, but one which Ignatius knew had the power to reform not only the Church of his day but also the world.

The sort of 'familiarity' Ignatius was concerned with is best expressed in images. Imagine an elderly wife and husband, sitting on rocking chairs on a verandah, saying very little to one another because there isn't much to say really, but still having a profound sense of being fully a part of each other's lives. Or imagine the kind of familiarity we have with old friends, whom perhaps we do not see very often, but who always remain the best of friends. Or imagine the familiarity a mother has with a young child, the unlaboured immediacy of the cuddle.

The hope for such familiarity was also a hope for a wonderfully integrated life. For instance, Ignatius was fond of asking people to use the so-called 'three powers of the soul' to meditate on the Gospels: memory, intellect and will. And behind this scholastic triad lay not just a device to get us more involved in a particular gospel story, but also a way to focus our entire beings on Jesus, a way of experiencing what it's like to be in synch with Jesus' passions, hopes, dreams, preferences. While Ignatius was realistic enough to know that, in this life, none of us ever reaches full purity of heart, he also knew that we can fleetingly feel what it's like to be at one with God's intentions for our world. Indeed, he expected us to be able to taste this inner consonance with the divine Spirit. The experience of this single-heartedness is at the heart of what is known as 'Discernment of Spirits'.

Discerning spirits

One of the more fascinating aspects of Ignatian spirituality is its emphasis on becoming aware of how we respond to God's presence. Taking a biblical theme, Ignatius speaks of discerning interior movements (spiritual or not-so-spiritual experiences). Indeed one of the terms most associated with Ignatian spirituality is discernment of spirits, which is the art of figuring out whether a particular feeling or attraction is leading us closer to God or further away from God.

Being in tune with God's will for us, with God's preferences for us, will generally be experienced as consolation – another important term in Ignatian spirituality. Experiencing consolation means different things at different times (and Ignatius has some tips on how to recognize consolation at different times), but generally speaking if we are discerning God's will correctly, we'll experience some sort of joy, peace, or a lack of tension in our prayer or in our lives. However, if we are considering something that is not of God, Ignatius expects us to recognize a kind of spiritual discomfort, tension, or even sadness, as we intuitively grasp that something may be drawing us away from intimacy with God. This latter experience is called desolation.

For some of us, such terms as 'discernment', 'consolation' and 'desolation' may sound so foreign that it is not apparent that we are already very familiar with the experiences behind these terms. For instance, anyone who has fallen in love has probably had an experience of consolation – the kind of glowing feeling accompanying thoughts of the one you love. Similarly, anyone who has felt the conflicts before doing something he or she knew was wrong is probably used to the experience of desolation – the kind of isolating feeling that results from having let down not only others but yourself as well.

A responsibility to discern

Ignatius liked appealing to our native reasonableness. It was obvious to him that if God is God, and if we are God's creatures, created for God's purposes, then God's purposes must be our purposes. It was equally obvious to him that if we acted according to God's purposes we should be fulfilled: to use more modern terminology, our beings would be integrated marvellously. What Ignatius brings to these 'reasonable' thoughts is the kind of passion such thoughts deserve. So it is not enough merely to seek God's purposes as one task among many; the seeking of God's purposes must be supremely important: no other goal is as worthy, no other goal can actually capture us as deeply as this can, because this goal is actually authored by God in the very core of our being. Similarly, if we are able to discern God's purposes, God's will for us, then doing God's will has to be our single most important commitment.

Not only does God reveal God's will to us in terms of an ongoing personal and corporate relationship with God, God has also revealed through Jesus what a life lived in absolute obedience to God's will looks like. Moreover, in Jesus, in his concrete historical life, we see what authentic discernment looks like; we see Jesus' own decisions; we catch glimpses out of the corners of our eyes (which is to say through the gospel-writers' and the early Church's eyes) of Jesus' own experience of consolation and desolation. That is why there is such an emphasis on Jesus' humanity in the Exercises and why the Gospels play such a pivotal role in Ignatian spirituality.

These few points are potentially spiritual dynamite. Ignatian spirituality is based on the theological conviction that God is in a direct person-to-person relationship with each of us, a relationship so real and so palpable that we can actually discover and follow God's particular will for us. For Ignatius, this is not just a possibility for the holiest of saints, but a practical necessity for all people. 'We were created to praise, reverence and serve God', Ignatius says, and we are to prefer whatever best allows us to fulfil that goal – something we do not decide so much as discover in the give and take of a day-to-day relationship with a God who will ever draw us closer and closer, if we would but learn to let ourselves be drawn.

The Holy Spirit and God's will for us

Arguably the most important thing in Ignatian spirituality is learning how to be aware of God's presence, learning how it feels to be in consonance with God's will, learning how it feels to be out of synch with God's will. Though Ignatius didn't speak of the Holy Spirit very often, all this talk of consolation and desolation could well be translated in terms of the Spirit: we have to let ourselves be taught how to become aware of the Spirit's groanings within us, what it feels like to act in accordance with these promptings, what it feels like to act against these promptings, and how to tell the difference between the Spirit's groanings and the other desires that seem to well up from deep within us.

Fortunately, Ignatius expected God to be the teacher. He fully expected God to lead us and to teach us how to recognize the divine voice (for instance, the person who guides another through the Spiritual Exercises is content with giving straightforward, matter-of-fact instructions, and lets God do the leading). And hundreds of years of experience of the Exercises have taught us that God does indeed lead. When people begin to pray, God teaches by giving us wonderfully consoling experiences when we're on the right track, and by leaving us with distinctly cold experiences when we're on the wrong track. Indeed, this is characteristic of many, if not all, of the great spiritual traditions in the Church.

3

The Ignatian World View

Central to understanding the Spiritual Exercises or Ignatian spirituality is entering into Ignatius' world view. His world view was theological, christological, strategic, and world affirming – arguably in the very best senses of all those terms.

A theological world view

First, Ignatius' world view is theological. For Ignatius, God is always and immediately active. The universe is held in being by God, and it is held in being very personally. This is not the remote Creator-God of more philosophical theology, but the God of love who demonstrates divine love by loving a universe into being, by working on behalf of all creatures, even by personally entering into the world for us, for me. The world is the privileged arena of divine blessing and divine revelation – something only appreciated in the light of discipleship with Jesus, 'who has become man for us', and so reveals the Father.

This God who acts immediately is Lord of all, and his lordship extends to my memories, my understanding and my will. In the Exercises, we are invited to offer these to God not because they are ours to offer, but because they are God's gifts and because they have been given to us to fulfil God's divine purposes. These gifts are directed by God, and God works just as immediately through and alongside these gifts as God does in the rest of creation. Our task is to allow ourselves to be directed by God, to learn how to recognize the promptings of the good Spirit, to learn to recognize the tell-tale signs of our listening to alternatives – whether generated by ourselves or others.

Thus the Ignatian world view is thoroughly theological – God is central and active, and God's divine activity intersects with ours. For God has preferences, and God communicates these preferences by offering our deepest desires and longings, by urging those longings into imaginative possibilities, by urging choice among these possibilities, and by drawing us to act according to our best choices. That God communicates these preferences with us is not a matter for speculation: in Jesus, those preferences are writ on the tableau of a human life lived precisely according to the logic of the Kingdom of God. The only matter for speculation is whether our relationship with God is actually changed by our choices, and whether those changes matter and are palpable. Ignatius knew they matter; he knew that what we choose affects our relationship with God. Discernment of spirits is a way of focusing on those palpable changes throughout the whole decision-making process. For him, true consolation is the fruit of closeness to God, which is in turn the fruit of being at one with God's will; and true desolation is nothing but the lack of such fruit, which is in turn the result of being at odds with God's will. Given that God is the author of our being, being at odds with God's will is to be at odds with our nature: 'for we were created to praise, reverence and serve God' (the First Principle and Foundation of the Spiritual Exercises).

A christological world view

Ignatius represents one of the high points of incarnational chris-
tology. He understood that Jesus, while completely and utterly
divine, revealed that divinity precisely through his humanity. And
we come to know the 'Lord and Master of All' by taking that revelation of God through Jesus' humanity dead seriously. For Ignatius,
'Jesus' is what God does in the world. Jesus is God's response to the
world. Jesus is how God addresses our inhumanity to one another,
our warring with one another, our deep-seated selfishness.

Ignatius was struck by the juxtaposition between the intensity
of what God did in the Incarnation and the unlikeliness of the
way God chose to do it. In his contemplation on the Incarnation,
Ignatius suggests that the retreatant flip back and forth between
God's concern for our planet and the events in Nazareth. How
does God plan to win over a planet bent on destroying itself
by hatred, violence and war? He graciously finds an unknown,
young, unwed woman named Mary in the middle of nowhere.
This is Ignatius' starting-point for his appreciation of what God
was doing in Jesus. It is his initial sense that God's ways are completely unlike our ways. It is his profound sense that the strategy
of the Kingdom of God is revolutionary and completely at odds
with the strategies by which most of the world operates.

Indeed, throughout the whole of the Exercises, there is a
constant harping back to this appreciation of God's strategy of
non-coercion, of incarnational solidarity with humanity. There
is a sense that God's will is to be done by doing what Jesus did:
by joining him and others in discipleship – a romantic but gutsy
and absolute commitment and attachment to the person of Jesus
in the midst of hardship, poverty and opposition. It is a strategy
that has but two things to commend it: one, it is God's preferred

strategy; and two, the strategy actually works and is absolutely compelling, when seen at play in Jesus' own historical life.

A strategic world view

Ignatius' world view was also strategic. What matters most is not understanding the world (though this is crucial), but deciding what to do with your understanding. In other words, what Ignatius appreciated is that the Christian life is fundamentally about action: action based on decisions, and decisions based on discerning God's will for us. To be concerned with God's will is of course to have opted for a strategic world view. In scriptural terms, the Ignatian world view is concerned most of all with love, with a love not expressed so much in words, as much as in deeds. Because loving is so important, loving well is important; and loving well means loving according to the exemplar of all love, according to the pattern of Jesus Christ.

While it is true to say that Ignatius' world view was dualistic and that it pitted good against evil, it would be truer to say that Ignatius pitted the strategy of good against the strategy of evil. What Ignatius was most concerned about was not rules or regulations, but where our decisions led us: either closer to God or away from God. The deception that good Christians are most susceptible to is the deception that seeming good is truly good, when in fact it leads slipperily away from God. The deception is not uncovered in the seeming good, but in the course, the sequence, the trail that leads from the initial choice to further choices, and finally to an end, which is not a thing so much as an alternative way of living: in more contemporary terms, the deception is the ways that patterns of life or lifestyles can seem so good but can end up dealing death in one way or another.

4

The Difference It Makes: Spirituality and the Goals of Ethics

Ethics is the study of how to choose among imagined, desirable, concretely possible alternative courses of action which, though grounded in present reality, promise some increase in the possibility of good emerging in the future. Christian ethics (as we use the term) is ethics which uses the person and life of Jesus as the norm for our decisions of what is possible. So, the question is, How do I let Jesus inform my imagination, my desires, my judgements of what is possible, what is feasible, what ought to be done in this particular case? In brief, the answer is: 'Get to know the person of Jesus through reading, praying, and studying the Gospels.'

The person of Jesus: some reminders from Chapter 1

The beauty of praying on the person of Jesus through the Gospels actually is its simplicity. It doesn't require years of spiritual training beyond the reach of any well-meaning Christian. It doesn't require mastery of weird or esoteric techniques. It doesn't require you to have already made long retreats. Fortunately enough, it requires only a heartfelt desire to know and love Jesus, a facility for what might be called day-dreaming, and a willingness to work with the Scriptures.

The latter point about the Scriptures is crucial. When we get right down to it, we have to admit that anything specific that we know about Jesus comes, one way or another, from the Scriptures, and most particularly from the Gospels. Everything else is an attempt to communicate the significance and the meaning of what we read there; but it never adds anything radically new; it never does a better job of revealing the person of Jesus. For this reason, a lot of Christian prayer is firmly grounded in Scripture. A lot of Christian prayer is designed simply to do what the Gospels were intended to do: namely, to reveal the person of Jesus.

Following Jesus requires some hard knowledge of how he actually lived, how he made decisions: you can't know Jesus without knowing something of his priorities, his activities, his commitments, his friends, his teachings, his hopes, his dreams, his heartaches. We need concrete data about Jesus so that our following Jesus can be equally concrete. And it must be tangible and real; it must affect our day-to-day decisions, as we said before, or are we saying, in effect, that Jesus is largely irrelevant to our lives?

Though Scripture does provide us with some hard data about who Jesus is, this is only useful if we recognize that the Risen Lord is the historical Jesus who walked in Palestine nearly 2000 years ago. They are one and the same person. When you stop and think about it, that's why we have kept the Scriptures intact over all these years; the Scriptures remain current and topical because the Jesus written about in the Gospels and the God written about throughout are alive today. Sad to say, but too many people neglect one of the fundamental beliefs of the Christian faith; namely, that Jesus is still fully and utterly a human being; he still has a personality and emotions; he can remember all the events written about him. Presumably, he is able to look back in fondness, recalling how his apostles messed up; he remembers what it feels like to be rejected (and he probably still feels its sting); he remains able to feel compassion for the poor and down-trodden; he perhaps still has a glint in his eye from laughing at the ways in which Peter always seemed to muddle everything up. The good news of the Resurrection is that Jesus, the very same Jesus his disciples knew and loved, that Jesus was raised up to life again, and that Jesus, the Jesus of the Gospels, is very much alive today. That same Jesus calls us to follow him.

Why is realizing that Jesus is still a human being that important? For one, were it not the case, we would be wasting our time reading and praying on the Gospels, for they would only be telling us who Jesus was, not who he is. The Gospels might then have some historical interest, but they would not be of any faith interest. Some people even fall into a bit of a trap: they leave the specifics of Jesus behind and try instead, with all the very best intentions, somehow to follow the Spirit. They may be wonderful and holy human beings, but they have missed a most wonderful opportunity to discover just how the Spirit of God actually moves people if they do not discover the Spirit alive in Jesus.

Another reason why realizing that Jesus is still a human being is important is that it makes following Jesus imaginable. For instance, a lot of Christians believe that Jesus is half human and half divine. Without realising it, they subtly reject the Church's teaching that the humanity of Jesus and the divinity never get mixed up, they don't sort of overlap. It is a historical fact that Jesus is as human as anyone else here and now. He will remain just as human forever. At the same time, in faith, we believe that this very human Jesus is so close to the Father that they are truly one in being.

How does this affect Christian ethics?

Well, if our Christian ethics is a discipleship of Jesus, and if we don't acknowledge that Jesus is truly human, that he was truly tempted like us in every way that we are tempted, that is, if we make him into a kind of superman with super powers unavailable to us so-called 'regular' human beings, then we will not follow him. We'll have the perfect excuse. In response to the hard teachings of Jesus, we'll respond something like this: 'Well, that's easy for you, Jesus, you're God, you're not like us. Now, if I were God, I'd follow you in a second. Why, it's not even fair to expect it of us.'

Some people get all worried when they hear someone stress the humanity of Jesus. They think it's suspicious-sounding. They think it's close to heresy or something. Chances are they are thinking that you have to keep the humanity and divinity somehow balanced, that stressing his humanity takes away from his divinity, makes it a 60-40 split or something. But the Church Councils and creeds are clear: Jesus is fully both. You can stress and stress Jesus' humanity until he's absolutely and utterly human in every way, and that's fine. In fact, the humanity of Jesus is the vehicle for the revelation of his relationship with God: so in a strange-sounding way, if you don't stress the humanity, the divinity disappears too.

So, to get to know Jesus, we have to read the Gospels. But once we start reading the Gospels, we begin to suspect that there are some problems. We may notice that the four Gospels don't really agree with each other all the time. We might wonder why one Gospel reports Jesus as having said, 'Blessed are the poor in spirit', while another has him simply saying, 'Blessed are the poor'. One Gospel has Jesus ruling out all divorce; another allows for exceptions on the basis of unchastity. After a while, it can seem as though no one could ever be sure of anything about Jesus.

The Gospels do admittedly differ from one another, and it would be a mistake to try to smooth out all the differences and weave them all into one seemingly more coherent account. But they differ because they really do tell legitimately different stories: different conversion stories, different appreciations of what was important, different ideas about how best to tell the story.

Just as we might want to ask a number of people about some-one or something to get as many points of view as possible, the Gospel writers present us with a rich and necessary diversity. No one person would have fully appreciated all that Jesus said, taught and did. No one person could have fully appreciated the meaning of Jesus' life. So the Gospels contain the early Church's cherished collection of the memories and experiences of those who knew Jesus best. Each Gospel then reveals a true and cru-cial side of Jesus' life and personality.

The important truth about Jesus seems not to be found by arguing the minutest details, nor by trying to figure out which Gospel passage is more accurate than the other. This is no doubt fascinating and remains very important in its own right, but it does not take away from the fact that the Gospels have another more primary purpose. We should let each Gospel do what it was meant to do: namely, make Jesus come alive, so that those who embrace these Gospels might get a genuine heartfelt sense of who Jesus was, so that they might get a real sense of who he is. The Gospel writers were not historians; they obviously didn't receive their information directly from heaven (otherwise, they would all have written exactly the same story). Instead, each writer recounted those incidents, stories, memories, myths, even some difficult-to-substantiate rumours that – as far as the Gospel writers were concerned, and as far as the early Church was con-cerned – best communicated what was important about Jesus, and the powerful impact he had on people's lives.

Scripture works: you can get to know Jesus from Scripture. The evangelists wrote the Gospels to communicate to us everything they thought was important for us to know about Jesus. Their being 'inspired' is our belief that they did this effectively, that Jesus' own spirit was with them as they were writing, so that they were writing from their own depths of experience. Not only do we believe that they and the early Church were imbued with Jesus' own spirit, we also believe that there is a sufficiency to the Gospels: they did not overlook anything of consequence. They didn't forget to communicate something that we just had to know if we were to make sense of Jesus' life. In other words, there is nothing of crucial importance about Jesus which is not in Scripture, though there admittedly were plenty of things which were not included in Scripture. That, for instance, is why the Church can confidently say that she believes that there will be no further public revelation. There is no need. We have had it all revealed. Jesus was the perfect and sufficient revelation of God, and Scripture makes that revelation of God, the person of Jesus, really present.

Without quoting chapter and verse, the Gospels present Jesus as having held to a particularly consistent strategy in both his teachings and actions, and a non-violent strategy at that. Though this strategy was evidently quite personal to Jesus, it also appears to have been based on Jesus' understanding of a larger divine strategy. For instance, Jesus understood God to have an unfailing and active desire for reconciliation. He also recognized God as exercising a providential care for the evil and unjust, no less than for the just. He further realized that this care effectively annulled claims that God punishes the 'wicked' through violence or misfortune. Indeed, Jesus' parables at times suggest a paradoxical and enduring preference, not only for the poor and downtrodden, but for sinners, for wrong-doers. Far from confronting evil with violence, with retribution, with punishment, or with destruction, Jesus often presents God as treating the sinner with care and solicitude. This attitude of Jesus, mirroring God's own attitude, must carry weight in Christian decision-making, in Christian ethics.

Similarly, at the heart of Jesus' teaching is an appreciation that God is more or less non-coercive. Frustrating though it may be, it is everywhere evident in our world that God does not use force to pressure compliance with the divine will. This seems to be corroborated in Jesus' own life inasmuch as he usually refrained from using force. Does this bear consideration in Christian decision-making? In social ethics? In political situations?

In both Matthew's and Luke's compilations of Jesus' ethical teaching, Jesus quite clearly enunciates a rule that we love our enemies, that we turn the cheek, that we return evil with good. At the same time, he unambiguously adduces a warrant for that rule: we must love our enemies because God does.

These passages afford us a rare glimpse of Jesus' own ethical discernment and discourse, one based not simply on discerning and doing God's particular will in a particular situation, but on discerning and incarnating God's attitudes, the divine strategy, as it were, in all of life's situations.

This non-coercive attitude of Jesus belongs to the heart of the Gospel. Consequently, it should be situated at the heart of Christian ethics. To date, it has not been asserted strongly enough.

Jesus' intention-actions were 'utterly human' in every way, while at the same time these self-same actions were God's activity in the world, as if to say that Jesus is what God was doing in our world. The Incarnation, considered as a symbol for the moment, not only points to God, but also says something about our world, about human life and its sacredness.

The divine strategy is interpreted for us by Jesus' life, from his birth through to the experiences of his resurrection which continue to this day. Indeed, theologically, we could argue that the symbol of the Incarnation is a symbol of this divine strategy: the Incarnation (along with Jesus' life, death, and resurrection) is part of the ultimate revelation of God's non-coercive, non-violent strategy, one entirely mind-boggling if taken to heart. Sadly, the Incarnation is often overlooked and not appreciated as being the quintessential divine response to all our warring, to all our violence, to our incredible ability to hurt one another in ways which must stretch even God's imagination; or, if it is not overlooked, it is considered to be ethically irrelevant.

Though it would be at least anachronistic, if not absurd, to attribute a theological appreciation of the later Christian symbol of the Incarnation to Jesus, still Jesus' life was lived in fidelity to this overall divine strategy. Our seeming inability ever really to accept Jesus' full humanity points to our reluctance to accept Jesus' consistent non-coerciveness and weakness. We refuse to see Jesus' life as a personal revelation of divine activity on our behalf. We hang on to images of a powerful God, when Jesus reveals the opposite. This has long affected our ethical decision-making.

The tension between the perduring belief in a God of Power and Might and the God Jesus revealed in weakness is also evident throughout Jesus' life. His temptations, for instance, while symbolically echoing the struggles of his people, nevertheless point to his personal struggle with power: 'Should I go it alone, meet my own needs? Should I take naked political power? Should I be the charismatic folk hero, play the pied piper, and overpower people's emotions by dazzling them to bits?' Instead he chose another route, the fourth temptation, as it were: he chose to work out of a small community, selecting 12 of the most unlikely persons he could find, financing his operation through the ministrations of women, throwing his lot in with his disciples and other followers, preaching the advent of God's reign – this 'fourth temptation' being the epitome of a non-violent, non-coercive strategy.

Trust in God

The heart of Jesus' teaching was a proclamation that God is and will always remain absolutely trustworthy. Jesus' listeners heard, in so many words, not once, but again and again, that they had nothing to lose by living as though God's reign were all that mattered: they could dare to love their enemies; they could dare to turn the cheek, return kindness for evil; they could dare to share their wealth, because – no matter what happened – God remained absolutely trustworthy. And though this eschatological edge has often been dismissed, living on that edge, living as though the Kingdom were literally within each person's grasp, rather than beyond reach – this was precisely what gave Jesus' ethical teachings their power and distinctiveness. It should also be clear that it was this distinct edge that made Jesus the threat he was: if God were seen to be truly of ultimate importance in people's immediate lives, if God were seen to be entirely trustworthy, if the prospect of death would no longer hold people in bondage, then people would be so free as to be potentially uncontrollable. Without the motivation of fear, the established order might be upset. Perhaps the Kingdom would actually come.

An appreciation of God's non-coercive, non-violent strategy vis-à-vis our world is essential for correctly discerning how to act under God's reign: viz., as active participants in building up God's Kingdom. Moreover, the strategy is so consistent on God's and Jesus' parts, that opposing strategies, despite seeming short-term benefits, ought to be counted as standing no possible chance for success: in other words, violent actions cannot build up the Kingdom. So we need 1) to trust God's ability to propose effective strategies for human action; 2) to trust Jesus' ability to discern and communicate those strategies; 3) to trust the effectiveness of the Gospels in communicating Jesus' fundamental intentions and desires; and 4) to trust that Christian communities can receive this communication and act upon it.

Discipleship and decisions

We began by suggesting that being a Christian entails a concrete following of Jesus of Nazareth, now Risen. We also noted that to follow Jesus requires solid knowledge of Jesus, that this requires that we know him inside out, and that this knowledge derives from our poring over his intentions and actions, that is, our getting to know Jesus as an agent. Once we begin to do so, and subject to the proviso that we accept Jesus' full humanity, we can begin to imagine concretely how to follow him.

All this presumes, of course, some desire to follow Jesus, and this desire is borne of an encounter with the Risen Jesus, an experience of having been invited to follow him, and this, quite personally. The response is faith, though the context of the experience of being invited to discipleship is also faith. Thus discipleship and spirituality go hand-in-hand.

At the same time, we argued that following Jesus requires decisions – it is the context in which a Christian faces ethical choices – but more than that, we need to see that our being Christians not only sets the context but also affects the method of ethics. There is a Christian ethics because there are distinctly Christian ways of making ethical decisions.

At the level of imagination, we are informed by the stories of Jesus' life: his commitments, his encounters with his contemporaries, his intentions, his actions. This has a direct impact on our ability to imagine alternative possibilities for action.

At the level of desire, we are imbued with the Spirit of Jesus which allows us to share Jesus' dreams, his hopes, his values, his passions. Without sharing his desires, we would not choose as he did. But sharing his desires is only possible in a faith relationship by which we become more and more united with Jesus, and being united with Jesus presumes a real encounter with Jesus, else there is no one to be united to. Again, ethics, the art of relating desire to decisions, becomes Christian ethics when the desires are born from union with Jesus Christ.

Even on the level of judgement, the actual decision-making stage, does our being Christian play a part, for all decisions, unless they are arbitrary, are based on criteria, and ethical criteria are known as ethical norms. Usually norms are considered laws, values, or methods, but Christians have a person as a norm: Jesus Christ. It is one thing to say we have Jesus as our norm, and another to actually treat him as a real norm; and to treat him as real norm means that we have to look for what was normative in his life. We have to look at how he made his decisions. Basically, we have to look for 'patterns' in Jesus' life, for what we have called 'strategies', to which he remained faithful. The fundamental strategy we have identified (though there could be many others) was acting upon a radical belief in God's ultimate trustworthiness. This is most evident in Jesus' teachings on non-violence, in his appreciation of God's non-coercive role in creation. A Christian, if he or she is intent on truly following Jesus, on truly being united with Jesus, will also share this strategy, and will make decisions accordingly.

Here it is important to realize that a Christian will consider Jesus as the norm for decision-making, not because this constitutes a new law, nor because Jesus should be mimicked, nor because a Christian might be incapable of making his or her own decisions, but rather because there has been an effective union with Jesus, a being filled with his Spirit, which results in shared desires, which in turn result in a shared strategy, which issue forth in shared decisions for shared goals.

Extracts from material produced in connection with his work for Concordia University, Montreal in the 1980s. See Further Reading, below.

5

Reading a Gospel with a Particular Focus: The Gospel of St Luke and Social Ethics

I set out below a method of praying on the Gospel of Luke with an eye to its social and ethical content. Though it is commonplace today to suggest that the Gospels ought to inform our ethical teaching, more often than not ethicians have used the Gospels as a source for ethical principles. But the Gospels are hardly candidates for such an approach. They were written, not as ethical handbooks, but as testimonies – testimonies of followers of Jesus, testimonies that were written, not so much to be studied as to be pondered, to be prayed over, to be celebrated, to be cherished.

The Incarnation and Nativity (Luke 1.26–80)

St Ignatius, the founder of the Jesuit order, brought a marvellous perspective to the Incarnation: he saw the event as having been the result of a very deliberate decision on God's part to save the world. As far as Ignatius was concerned, the world was in a deadly historical cycle of violence and self-destructive behaviour, and God quite literally decided to do something about it.

This may not strike anyone as having been a revolutionary insight, but the beauty of praying on Scripture, as opposed to simply reading it, is the time available to sit with the Incarnation, to imagine oneself practically within the mind of God, working out the various ways one might save the world (i.e. floods, threats and warnings, shows of strength), and then to be flabbergasted, even overcome, by the sheer improbability of the way God went about changing the trajectory of world history. More than that, the time spent in prayerful reflection allows us to savour the almost imperceptible but nonetheless sure mark of the divine precisely in the unlikeliness, the smallness, the weakness, the riskiness, of the event. One senses immediately the powerful impact of God's ways being so unlike our ways. One begins to get a feel for the way God does things. One even begins to sense that God's ways, though remaining thoroughly mysterious on one level, are nonetheless singularly attractive, peculiarly beautiful, and remarkably compelling. The divine strategy delicately roots itself in our hearts.

How to pray this passage

I might begin by trying to feel as deeply as possible the pain, the suffering, the self-destructiveness, the longing, the hoping of the world 2000 years ago. Then, I would, as Ignatius suggested, seesaw back and forth between God's desire to do something about the mess we were in, and the theological narratives surrounding Jesus' conception and birth in Luke's gospel. I would be careful not to get bogged down in questions of whether it happened the way Luke reported it; for Luke wanted, more than anything else, to try to drive home the early Church's belief that Jesus' conception and birth were, in a most profound sense, to be understood in terms of God's action in history.

Unless there is some feeling of genuine attraction to God's way of bringing about salvation, the ethical import of these passages will invariably be rejected. God quite particularly chose the powerless and the weak, the marginalized and scandalous, to achieve the divine purpose. But do we expect the same? Or do we look to power as the chief vehicle of change in our world? God did not use violence to bring about change. Are we content to nod approvingly to the occasional (or even systematic) use of violence to sustain social order? In other words, are we content to follow a different strategy than God? Are we so sure of ourselves that we spurn God's ways and choose violence, power, or prestige? What do we know that God doesn't know?

The hidden life (Luke 2.39–52)

We know very little of Jesus' hidden life – the period between his birth and baptism. To some, this is bothersome, yet for others, it is entirely fortuitous; for the lack of detail suggests a very important insight: nothing spectacular occurred in Jesus' early life. It was entirely ordinary. When people gathered after his death and told the usual wake-stories, we can presume that no one could recall anything extraordinary from Jesus' youth except for his Bar Mitzvah at the temple in Jerusalem.

How to pray this passage

For the hidden life, it often helps to spend a few prayer hours imagining how ordinary and unspectacular Jesus' early life must have been. Though we have few details, we can 'work our way backwards', as it were: we know how Jesus turned out in later life, so we can ask ourselves why Jesus was so compassionate to the poor. What kinds of experiences might Jesus have had which might account for this sensitivity? Jesus seemed singularly able to trust God: why was this the case? How do people generally learn to trust? Did Jesus have those sorts of experiences?

In a very real sense, we will be 'making this all up', using our imaginations. But we are hardly dealing with pure fantasy, or at least not necessarily so. One of the chief uses of the imagination is to make things conceivable, to make things really imaginable: in other words, to represent reality. Thus, when we use our imaginations to give Jesus a normal, very ordinary past, we are doing nothing more than trying to be present to the reality of Jesus' actual ordinariness: we are trying to make him a little more real, a little more imaginable, a little more 'like us in all things but sin'.

The ordinariness of Jesus' first 30 years should give us pause. Jesus was not born into wealth, into privilege. He didn't enjoy access to the best schools. He didn't rub shoulders with the political leaders and yet, by the very ordinary processes of human learning and human living, he was able to discern God's purposes most clearly. Without any social advantages, he was able to make an impression on our world unlike anyone before or since.

Where do we look for our present-day prophets? Do we really believe the poor have something to say to the rest of us? Or do we use our degrees, our positions, our contacts as a buffer between ourselves and those whose lives are so ordinary that they are anonymous? How do our structures – social, economic, ecclesiastical – 'listen' to these ordinary people? How do wealthy countries hear the poorer countries? Where is God speaking today? Through whom?

Social ethics is about imagining possibilities for the future; but it is also more than that: it is about concrete strategies of the imagination aimed towards actions. These imaginative strategies aim at fulfilling desires, but the ordinariness of Jesus' life can help us to realize that there are millions of other ordinary people whose desires are not met by the present-day political, economic, social and religious strategies of the imagination. Could Jesus have had the same desires had he come from a more privileged background? Is there a logic of the poor, one which merits a privileged place in our strategizing for change?

The Baptism (Luke 3.21–2)

Luke's account depicts Jesus in prayer after his baptism. It is not clear whether the others present heard the voice. Nevertheless, by situating the event in the context of prayer, Luke clearly presents the incident as a powerful religious experience on Jesus' part. As a religious experience, the words heard were heard in the depths of his being. Rather than receive a clear directive from God to do something or other, Jesus' experience was bald and simple: Jesus had an experience of being loved to bits by God.

It is fascinating to consider why Jesus wanted to be baptized. Luke is silent on the question, but it makes some sense to consider that Jesus wanted to receive baptism because he felt he *needed* to receive baptism. Far too often, we follow Matthew's lead, and conclude that Jesus was just setting a good example – almost pretending (if we can put it that way) to do what the others were all doing. The others were repenting with all seriousness, but Jesus – or so the conventional wisdom goes – hardly needed to repent. So what was he there for? I would suggest that perhaps he was there because he experienced some real responsibility for the sin of this world. This might sound shocking to some, but the Jewish conception of corporate guilt suggests that Jesus, like any other good Jew, would have felt and taken responsibility for the sins of the whole people. Thus, even though we say that Jesus remained without sin, this cannot be taken to mean that Jesus never experienced real guilt, sorrow, and a need for repentance. Newer insights on social sin, on our corporate responsibility for sinful social structures, would corroborate this ancient approach to sin.

How to pray this passage

For the baptism, I would suggest that we face this controversial question head on, by wondering what this experience might have meant to Jesus. It is not particularly helpful to see this as an affirmation of his divinity. The baptism seems to have had a much more immediate impact on Jesus' concrete, historical life.

I would suggest that we approach the baptism from the context of Jesus leaving home, his leaving Mary, his moving on. Imagine him being nervous and unsure of the next step, his having been bothered for years by an irksome desire and need to take a new direction in his life. Imagine him feeling challenged to do something about sin, about evil. Imagine him realizing that he is a real part of this sinful and self-destructive world. And imagine him wanting to be cleansed, to experience new life, new hope.

It is crucial to appreciate that Jesus probably needed to be affirmed by God. In this light, we might make some connections with our own vocation histories, appreciating how God has confirmed our life decisions, and then we can consider Jesus' baptism as a confirmation of his growing sense of vocation. I don't think it would be a mistake even to approach Jesus' baptism as a conversion experience for Jesus: not a conversion in terms of sin, per se, but a conversion in terms of a being grasped and turned by God. Not to allow Jesus to experience such profound human experiences of grace is severely to limit his participation in humanity: to that extent we tragically make him 'unlike us in all things'.

That Jesus probably experienced guilt and responsibility, not for his own personal sins, but for the social sin of his world, is, of course, significant for us. It corresponds to an almost universally Christian conviction that repentance and confession go together – even for Jesus.

Moreover, the baptism suggests that repentance is hardly reducible to regret over personal sins. Rather, true repentance – the kind Jesus himself would have experienced – is a communal affair. It is ourselves taking communal responsibility for the world we have created. The baptism of Jesus contains the seeds of a promise for all of us: namely, that, inasmuch as God communicated palpable divine approval to Jesus in his moment of repentance and conversion, so too we ought to expect much the same. Indeed, we can put it more strongly: without an experience of God's love, without hearing God say 'Trust me!' in the core of our being, we will not have any basis for real hope. Without hope, commitment vanishes, and possibilities become the wisp of vapid fantasy.

The temptations (Luke 4.1–13)

Evidently, the baptism was an unsettling experience for Jesus. Fine, God loved him, but what was he to do next? God didn't say. And so, immediately following his conversion experience, Jesus was 'led by the Spirit' to the wilderness to be tempted.

Conversions are like that. While wonderful, they pull the rug right out from under us. Being grasped in love by love changes everything. Priorities are challenged. Cherished ideas become suspect. All things become possible, but that tends to be confusing, to say the least. Enthusiasm risks becoming uncritical. Messiah complexes seem natural. Powerful religious experiences risk being personalized into nothingness. In short, conversions invariably bring us to confront our own demons.

The power of Jesus' temptations evaporates unless we believe Jesus was truly tempted. In other words, these temptations do not come from 'outside' Jesus so much as they represent his own desires, his own demons as it were. There is no temptation unless there is personal desire. In retreat settings, I often tell people of the absolute aversion I had to Brussels sprouts as a child. The fact is no one could have tempted me to do anything in return for the promise of a Brussels sprout. They could have promised me all the Brussels sprouts in the world in exchange for my moving a fork one inch but it wouldn't have worked. Unless a temptation arouses a real and personal desire, there is no temptation.

The same goes for Jesus' temptations. Unless he actually desired what he was tempted by, there were no temptations. If the temptations were experienced as despicable evil taunts by Satan, there would have been no real temptations. But we know the temptations were real. We know that Jesus struggled day and night for what must have seemed like an eternity against these temptations – these desires which he himself held in his heart.

Thus it is important to consider each temptation, asking ourselves what Jesus might have found attractive in them, wondering why he decided not to act on these desire-temptations, why he chose to act ultimately on other desires.

Upon examination, it would seem that each temptation revolves around 'strategic' questions of how to respond to the powerful experience of his baptism. Should he take God's approval and savour it, turn it into his own private treasure? In other words, should he turn symbolic stories into symbolic bread, use his blessedness to meet his own needs? Evidently, he was able to see through that temptation; evidently, he had other desires vying for his heart. And so, rather than pursue a life of gratuitous self-seeking, his attention was turned to the Kingdom – a proclamation of the blessedness, not just of Jesus, but of all humanity.

How should he proclaim this in-breaking of the Kingdom of God? Should he take political power? Accept the demonic offer of dominion over all the kingdoms of the world? Should he simply make all the decisions for everyone, craft a worldly kingdom into the Kingdom of God? He could have arguably made better decisions than anyone else, so it must have been tempting. It's crucial to realize that Jesus was really tempted to use power, to coerce, to limit freedom, even at the cost of disempowering everybody else. He felt this as an attractive possibility, he may even have relished the idea – at least for a while. But that would have meant usurping all communal responsibility for the Kingdom. Perhaps even more telling, building the Kingdom by a personal exercise of power would have meant that others would not base their actions on an experience of being loved by God. How could he use his baptism, his experience of the outpouring of God's Spirit, as his grounds for inaugurating the Kingdom if he were not willing to let others do the same?

The third temptation is subtle. The symbol is jumping off the parapet of the temple and tempting God to save him. While the presumptuousness of the idea is immediately apparent, there is also a hidden temptation: namely to wield charismatic power over people's minds and hearts.

Can you imagine the stir were Jesus to jump off the highest point of the temple, in full view of all the people who normally would have crowded the temple on any given day? A spectacular trick like that would have translated into immediate hero-worship. Jesus would have had them all in the palm of his hand. He could have played the Pied Piper, seducing them to follow him out of enchantment for this expression of unbelievable power. In effect, this third temptation is not unlike the second: it too is an abuse of power, the usurping of the role of divinely authored conversion as the vehicle for real change.

You might wonder about Jesus' other miracles. Despite attempts this past century to explain away all the miracles, no one seriously doubts that Jesus performed many miracles. While extraordinary, they were hardly tricks. Instead, Jesus' miracles were all works of compassion; and people were moved to amazement, not at what Jesus had done, but by what God had done. Those who experienced miraculous healings, for instance, always went away 'praising God', not praising Jesus. It is not clear how Jesus made it apparent to everyone that he was not himself responsible for the miracles; yet he did so. He refused to wield personal charismatic power; and when people were inclined to gush over him, he aptly rebutted that, with only a smidgen of faith, everyone can do greater works than he.

How to pray this passage

For the temptations, it is important first of all to keep focused on Jesus: they are first of all *his* temptations, not ours. We might wonder why he was 'driven' to the desert, what it was about the baptism experience that sent him to the desert, what he was trying to work out. Then, I would suggest that we actively imagine Jesus being pulled and tugged by his competing desires to really take the bull by the horns and get the Kingdom on the road. Let his temptations be real, let him struggle, let him be deceived, and then let him see the hand of God even more clearly afterwards.

After we begin to appreciate the power and depth of those desires in Jesus' heart, we might let ourselves be struck by the utter implausibility of his decision to proclaim the Kingdom by living in a small, roving community, composed of the most unlikely persons any of us could ever imagine. After all, this is precisely the strategy that won out in the end. Does this have ethical import? Should this influence our actions?

Though we have suggested that we first consider these temptations as Jesus' own, we can be quite sure that these temptations are as strong today as then. What is the status of these temptations in our own age? Have we all become political realists, or are we capable of seeing through the deceits of power, of prestige, of selfishness? More importantly perhaps, what do we think of Jesus' strategy – his choosing to live out his ministry in a small community of less-than-impressive individuals? Do we think that strategy has anything to commend it? Was Jesus correct in thinking that this was the best way in his time to accomplish what God had seemingly wanted him to accomplish? Who in our world is hearing and proclaiming the same message? NATO? Our economic gurus? Our politicians? The Christian Base Communities? Parish support groups? Groups like Oxfam and Tools for Peace? Are we willing to opt for Jesus' strategy wholeheartedly? Or do we have reservations? Where do we expend our most energy in life? Following Jesus' strategy? Where do questions of ultimacy arise in our lives? Are we uncomfortable to let ourselves be defined by such religious aspirations and strategies? Is the challenge of communally following Jesus the challenge of our lives, or have we been caught up in the tangled web of our culture's insatiable quest for economic, social, political, psychological and religious self-sufficiency?

Preaching in Nazareth (Luke 4.14–30)

Interestingly enough, Luke places Jesus' return home almost immediately after his baptism and temptations. Luke is stressing, more clearly than the other evangelists, that Jesus met opposition from the very outset of his ministry. In other words, there never was a golden age to Jesus' preaching, no time when he was unambiguously accepted. No, Jesus was subject to misunderstanding and outright opposition at every turn: from his conception, through his public ministry, to his death, and beyond that after his resurrection.

It's important not to downplay the effect this opposition would have had on Jesus. No one enjoys rejection. In Luke's account, Jesus has just left the desert, presumably with a lovely glint in his eye, a wonderful grasp of his Father's will, a clearer sense of his role, a keen insight into the divine strategy, an infectious exuberance. In short, he would have been in a state of profound consolation. And so, with all the excitement he could have mustered, he proclaimed Isaiah's message, one which summed up his own sense of mission; but he didn't get the reaction he had hoped for. He had proclaimed the Jubilee Year, the year when social inequities would be resolved, when wealth would be levelled out. He proclaimed good news for the poor, which would have been good news for the rich too, had they been concerned for the poor. But nobody noticed. Nobody cared. So he turned on them harshly. Problems immediately developed. His very life was endangered.

In Matthew's gospel, we read that Jesus only turned on the people after they had insulted him; but in Luke's gospel we read that the people were amazed at his gracious words, that he won the approval of all. Luke leaves the impression that this response of approval and amazement was what angered Jesus. It was as though his wonderfully but extremely challenging message went in one ear and straight out the other. They refused to appreciate what God was up to, what God had been up to all along. Religion was a salve for them. It gave them pleasure; and now and then they even fancied the diversion of being dazzled by a particularly earnest reading of the scrolls. And Jesus was infuriated.

How to pray this passage

I would try to imagine Jesus' excitement in returning home, the initial enthusiasm of the people receiving him, and their sense of something powerful having happened to Jesus, their pride that a hometown boy had all the neighbouring towns talking. I would let all of this affect Jesus. But then I would try to appreciate the other events as they unfolded, trying to understand why Jesus seems to have brought opposition upon himself by his own comments. I would pray to feel his dejection, to share his feelings. I would try to figure out why he turned on his own town, why they turned on him. I would especially take some time simply to be with Jesus in his disappointment. I would wonder how he reacted. Did he kick himself afterwards for what he said? Had he foreseen the reaction of the people? Had he considered all of this in the wilderness? Did he begin to second-guess himself? Did he pray to the Father? What might he have said?

One important little note. Some translations almost suggest that Jesus was protected by some miraculous intervention when he slipped through the crowd. The Greek original does not support such a reading. Indeed, it suggests something quite different: it portrays Jesus as having walked right through the middle of the crowd, yet nobody dared to touch him. This seems to be suggesting, not a miracle, but a respect on the crowd's part for the authority Jesus wielded in his very person, an authority which gave them pause. For now.

That said, this passage is dynamite, ethically speaking. The Jubilee year required that people free all their slaves, that they redistribute their wealth and land, giving lands to widows and orphans. They had to cancel all of their debts, and they had to return any land to anyone who had had to sell their land previously to get out of debt. In short, the Jubilee year was a kind of social pressure valve, a vehicle for ensuring that social inequities didn't continue for very long.

As might be expected, there never was a real, full-blown Jubilee year in Israel. You can well imagine how unpopular such an event would have been for those 'blessed' with lots of land and wealth. And yet Jesus saw it as something very attractive. He loved the idea of the Jubilee Year, and he proclaimed it as good news indeed. But the people simply applauded his wonderful words, they gushed with pride at this fine young son returned home. Sad to say, but they didn't hear a word he said. And so he turned on them, getting them so infuriated in turn that they wanted to kill him.

But what of Jesus' dream? Can we share the same dream? Are we attracted by the possibility (remote though it may seem) of a world in which social inequities are levelled out? Would we be willing to sacrifice much so that others might have a little more? What is stopping us? How deep is our desire to follow Jesus? What are our priorities? Our fears? Can we imagine ourselves in Jesus' congregation that day? What would we have done? How do we respond when we, in our present-day congregations, hear this and other radical passages read? Would Jesus turn on us too?

Cure of Simon Peter's mother-in-law (Luke 4.38–44)

This is also a fascinating story. It invites the whole question of Jesus' miracles. Did Jesus do wondrous things by exercising his own power, or are they expressions of the Father's power? Was

Peter correct in Acts when he said that God worked the miracles through the man Jesus (Acts 2.22 ff)? Was Jesus correct when he said that his followers would be able to do greater things than he? Does that mean the miracles are not manifestations of Jesus' personal divine power, but are instead manifestations of God's power to act through us? These questions are important inasmuch as they affect how we approach Jesus' humanity.

Perhaps even more important is the stress Jesus himself places on the proclamation of the Kingdom: the proclamation is more important than any healings, an attitude which suggests that the healings were themselves proclamations of the Kingdom, extraordinary signs of God's always-present love and care.

How to pray this passage

I might try to imagine myself living in that time when Jesus arrived. I would ask myself how I would have reacted had I heard there was a real healer down the street – not a charlatan, but a real healer, who had cured several people I knew very well. I would let my own hurts (psychological and physical) come to mind, and I might imagine myself seeking after Jesus. I might be healed, or I might have been one of the ones who went after Jesus the next morning, begging him to stay. In any event, it would be important to have some sense of Jesus' commitment to his mission of proclaiming the Kingdom, how that was more important than my being healed. This perspective is crucial, and simply 'knowing it' is only half the battle, for actually appreciating its significance is necessary to understand Jesus' passionate commitment.

I might ask myself whether I, like Jesus, am ultimately committed to bringing about the Kingdom. What of my religious attitudes? Do I pray to God only when I want something? When

I want to be healed of some hurt in my life? When I want God to do something to fix something in my life or my world? The folk in Simon Peter's town had a faith like that. They couldn't believe that Jesus would leave their town. They wanted him to pray for them some more. They wanted him to fix things for them. But he said no. He had something more important to do.

The call of the first disciples (Luke 5.1–11)

This is a wonderful story, full of drama, and dialogue, and rich images. The chief character, after Jesus of course, is Simon Peter; and we are offered a first glimpse of Simon's penchant for the dramatic gesture. Here, he protests that Jesus leave him alone because of his sinfulness.

Many things could be said about that incident, but most significant perhaps is Jesus' seeming disregard for Simon's sinfulness, his refusal to let Simon use his sinfulness as an excuse not to follow him. In response to Simon's plea, 'Leave me Lord, I am a sinful man', Jesus says, 'Do not be afraid. I will make you a fisher of men'. Jesus does not even address the sinfulness as sinfulness, and instead names it as fear.

How to pray this passage

I would imagine myself in Simon Peter's place, or as one of the other apostles observing the events as they unfolded. I might ask myself whether I use my sinfulness or unworthiness as an excuse not to follow Jesus. Would I feel what Simon Peter felt that day? Have I ever told the Lord – in one way or another – that I'm not good enough to follow him, that I'm too weak, that I'm not faithful enough, not reliable enough? I might wonder how Jesus would have reacted. Like Jesus reacted to Simon Peter?

We religious types are inclined to blame all the world's evils on sin. We are also tempted to a mock humility, protestations of our smallness and insignificance – and we repeatedly use these excuses to avoid the hard work of the Kingdom. Leave me, Lord, for I'm having too tough a time with daily life. Leave me, Lord, for I'm very ordinary. Leave me, Lord, because others can do a better job than I. Leave me, Lord, for I am too sinful.

Jesus would not be inclined to accept such excuses. Fear is crippling. Kierkegaard called it the *sickness unto death*. And death it is, for fear is the enemy of hope. Fear is a refusal to let God's love penetrate and be effective. Fear is disbelief in the power of Jesus' strategy to bring about effective change. Fear is idolatry, letting ourselves believe that God is not completely trustworthy, that we have to hang on to something or someone else for our dear lives. At the same time, Jesus did not simply say 'Don't be afraid' to Simon; he also made a promise: *I will make you a fisher of men.*

The solution to crippling fear is the promise. Jesus was no stranger to fear, but neither was he a stranger to God's promise. His baptism in God's love emblazoned that promise in his heart. He did not so much *make* a promise as he *shared* a promise: the same one he experienced.

How much of what we human beings do is in response to fear? The danger, of course, is that we respond to fear by trying to control the future, by sticking to the familiar, by limiting possibilities for change. We effectively block the Kingdom at every turn, for the Kingdom means change; it means new relationships; it means embracing a perspective of ultimacy; it means living a life of radical trust; it costs a certain willingness to live in a world of indeterminacy. How often do we despair of the efficaciousness of care, trying instead to become paragons of self-sufficiency, securing our futures, avoiding all risk? Are we more liable to respond to the lack of care in our socio-economic-political-religious structures by looking after ourselves first, or does the lack of caring structures embolden us to action? Honestly, how central is fear in our lives? Or do we find ourselves so secure in ourselves that we don't need to fear, simply because we don't need care?

The cure of the paralytic (Luke 5.17–26)

While the story is visually very dramatic, it is also a story of desire and persistence, if not on the paralytic's part, at least on the part of his friends who lowered him through the roof to Jesus' feet. Interestingly enough, it is this great desire and persistence which Jesus counts as faith, a faith so strong that Jesus forgives the paralytic's sins immediately.

I suspect that the most significant aspect of this event is the seeming fact that Jesus forgave the paralytic's sins without requiring any demonstration of prior sorrow. Most of us were taught that to be forgiven, not only had we to be truly sorrowful, but we had to hold a firm resolution to try not to sin again. Yet Jesus' forgiveness seems unconditional. Jesus doesn't forgive the paralytic because the paralytic wants to be forgiven – there is no indication of that whatsoever. Rather, Jesus forgives the paralytic because he, Jesus, wants to, because Jesus had this desire, a desire which sprang up in his heart when he was confronted with the faith of the paralytic's friends.

How to pray this passage

Many people use their imaginations and see themselves as the paralytic, envisioning themselves as bound and unable to move, then being lowered and set down at Jesus' feet. Others might find this too busy, and instead they might simply want to focus on a moment in the narrative – say, on Jesus' spontaneous desire to forgive the paralytic. They might simply want to sit with Jesus' desire, a desire which we can affirm as continuing to this day, and let his desire to forgive affectively and effectively transform them.

A number of the passages above can be used for an extended meditation on personal sinfulness, on the reality of all types of sin and on our complicity in it. Some people approach these passages as a type of reality therapy: in the intimacy and privacy of prayer, we can have a good, long, honest and hard look at our lives. We can look for the ways we repeatedly get snared; we try to identify our Achilles' heel, our ethical character flaw (in a Shakespearean sense) – in a phrase, at our very real, historical, palpable need of a Saviour.

When praying on sinfulness, we are invited to encounter the utter emptiness of sin, the lie of self-sufficiency proclaimed by sin, the perversity of sin's ability to twist our most beautiful and divinely-authored desires into self-service, the malevolence of our world's penchant for distorting vulnerability into fear and thence to sin. Eventually we will wonder why we persist in sinning when every chord of our body pines for a relationship with God. At the same time, face-to-face with the utter absurdity of sin, we accept the fact that nevertheless we sin. At this point, we know something of what St Paul was talking about in his Letter to the Romans, where he spoke of sensing a different law, a law of sin, working within him. Neither St Paul nor anybody since could or ever will find a solution to that problem apart from receiving the free gift of salvation offered by Jesus Christ: 'Who will deliver me from this wretched body of death?' St Paul cried. 'Thanks be to God, through Jesus Christ our Lord; we have a Saviour' (Rom. 7.24–5).

For all that, praying on sinfulness should not leave us mired in the bog of our sinfulness. Quite to the contrary, for the virtually universal result of healthy prayer on sinfulness is a profound awareness of just how much we are unconditionally loved and accepted by God. None of us deserves salvation. None of us can hold his or her head up in innocence. And yet we are saved. We can't earn it; we can't increase it or decrease it; we are simply loved immeasurably and eternally. Such love devastates; it unsettles; it is more powerful than all the sin we could ever imagine. Such is the experience of bringing our sinfulness to God, that we experience an indescribable freedom when we open ourselves to the efficaciousness of God's freely given forgiveness. Quite simply, despite the focus on sin (but actually because of how sin is focused upon), the foretaste of salvation characteristic of prayer on sinfulness is most freeing and sublime.

The problem is that only the scrupulous enjoy focusing on sin. In elections, people will vote for those who ignore social sin and proclaim greatness instead. People are so used to being hammered by sin and guilt, that they have never experienced the freeing aspects of admitting sinfulness. Instead, they hang on to mistaken beliefs that, in some way or another, they deserve salvation. Because they think they deserve it, salvation is not experienced as a wondrous gift, but this comes back to haunt them; for, if salvation is based on our just desserts, then we are always standing in fear and trembling – not before the tremendousness of God's majesty, but before a God who is bent on judgement. God is no longer the father of the prodigal son, the shepherd of the lost sheep, the God who forgave Israel again and again and again. We feel we have to earn God's acceptance, and we secretly – or not so secretly – fear God's rejection. Fear takes root and festers, imperceptibly but just as insidiously distorting our lives.

During prayer, we might let ourselves be struck by how irrelevant and pointless all of this talk about unconditional love and forgiveness is in much of our lives. We might look around at our world, and see where any of this seems significant. Isn't it odd that the drama of salvation, our being loved unconditionally by God has seemingly nothing to do with how we structure our lives together? What difference does belief in such a God make? If you are in business, what difference would it make if you believed, not simply that God loves you unconditionally, nor even that God loves everyone so, but that this is the most important thing in the universe? Does faith make a difference? Does it make a concrete difference at the level of our decision-making? What would our world look like if everyone really believed in such a God? This is not idle speculation, for Jesus didn't preach much more than this: Love God and, because God loves your neighbour, love your neighbour too. Love God and because God loves your enemy, love your enemy too. If this is the core of Jesus' teaching, is it really significant? Does it make a difference as it should? Or was Jesus piously deluded, a religious fanatic whose teaching hardly suffices to deal effectively with today's world?

The Great Sermon (Luke 6.20–36)

I think it important to see how consistent the Beatitudes are with Mary's Magnificat, with God's strategy in the Incarnation, with Jesus' choice in the desert, with his selection of Isaiah's passage in the synagogue, with his choice of the apostles. Again, in seeing that his Father blesses the poor, the hungry, the sorrowful, the hated, the outlawed, Jesus turns things on their head. He confronts the world's estimation of value, and suggests that God's calculus of value is radically different from our own.

This is especially evident in verse 28 where Jesus asks his disciples to love their enemies, to do good to those who hate them, to turn the other cheek when they are struck. Why? Because God is kind to the ungrateful and the wicked, and we must be likewise.

Especially worthy of note is verse 46: 'Why do you keep calling me "Lord, Lord" and never do what I tell you?' The Christian churches have largely ignored Jesus' hard teachings on non-violence and love of enemy. Why? I suspect that it is something to do with our inability to imagine a world in which Jesus is taken that seriously. In other words, we are not entirely sure whether we trust Jesus' strategy. At times, it sounds as though we're actually begging to differ from Jesus.

How to pray this passage

The passage is quite long, and the practical ramifications of what Jesus said are so massive that it is easy to get lost in the prayer, spending more time solving problems than attending to the Lord himself. However, if you have never done so, you can do a lot worse than spend a few prayer periods asking yourself whether you agree with Jesus. Do you agree with his seemingly thorough-going stance of non-violence? Or do you disagree with Jesus, thinking that sometimes it's all right to kill our enemies instead of loving them, okay to return evil for evil, instead of good for evil. Or perhaps you may think that we have to find some other way of understanding these passages. If you find yourself at odds with what Jesus seems to have said on this or other points, it might be good to imagine Jesus preaching, and imagine yourself actually interrupting him, protesting that you don't think he's correct, or insisting that he couldn't possibly want us to take these things literally, and then let it go on from there.

You might want to believe Jesus, but you might also be hon-est enough to admit (with most of the rest of us) that you don't quite see it his way yet. You may imagine yourself going to Jesus after the sermon and asking him to explain things for you a bit.

Whether you agree with Jesus or not, a marvellous way of praying the Beatitudes (and the whole Sermon, for that matter) is initially to focus on Jesus' personage, rather than his words per se. The importance of what Jesus is saying is dependent on the fact that this is his vision, this is his sense of what really matters, this is his appreciation of the divine strategy. In other words, it might be a mistake to consider his teachings from a narrow, logical or practical point of view alone, as if Jesus having said these things was beside the point, as if the words stood alone. Thus you may want to beg the Lord to help you to appreciate the beauty of his vision, to see whether and why non-violence might be preferable, and to see it with your entire being rather than with your practical intellect alone. You might beg the Lord to help you actually to become enthralled and caught up with his vision of how things should and could be, to appreciate the beautiful dream which fuelled Jesus' teachings.

In some sense, this is the heart of the gospel. Biblical scholars argue that the Great Sermon was not a real sermon: what we have inherited is a collection of various teachings from throughout Jesus' public life. Because they are a compilation, they're even more crucial: in effect, they are a conscious summary, a focused recollection, of the major points of Jesus' ethical teaching. They should not be lightly dismissed.

And yet, we have largely dismissed them. Centuries ago, the Church made a distinction between counsels and precepts. The counsels were viewed as invitations, where the precepts were viewed as obligatory commands. The distinction was made on the basis of the teaching on celibacy, where Jesus clearly suggests that celibacy is a gift not given to all. The radical teachings of the Great Sermon were relegated to the same counsel category. Thus while it would be laudable for someone to embrace radical love of neighbour and non-violence, still it, like chastity, was not necessary: one could be a good Christian while holding a different position.

The problem is that the two cases are hardly parallel. Celibacy is nowhere suggested as a command, but love of enemy is. Because celibacy is a gift, so too marriage is a gift: without the gift of celibacy, God's particular will is a call to the married life. But if a call to love of enemy is a gift, then we would have to argue – at least if we are to remain consistent – that a call not to love our enemies would likewise be a gift, a particular vocation. Happily, most minds recoil at such a suggestion.

The challenge of Jesus' teachings, a challenge to be faced in prayer and action, is precisely whether we are willing to follow Jesus this far. We should be convinced that, if Jesus' strategy is non-violent, any other competing strategies will end up being ineffectual. So long as we think that good can be pursued through violent means, we are succumbing to the lure of short-term gain. Violence is a short cut for those who do not believe in the power of grace and conversion.

The sinful woman (Luke 7.36–50)

The woman in this story is not Mary Magdalene. In fact, we are not told her name at all. Again, this is a very graphic narrative, one which lends itself to use in an imaginative type of prayer.

One of the things which I find most striking is the way in which Luke seems to have deliberately focused on the tools of this woman's work as the instrument of her devotion to Jesus. For instance, the tears, which might well have been used to feign affection in other circumstances, are here redeemed by a great outpouring of authentic love. She brings myrrh, a perfume used under other circumstances to entice people, but here used to anoint Jesus. She kisses Jesus' feet, her kisses again having been used elsewhere under different conditions. She dries Jesus' feet with her hair, long hair having been one of the chief signs of beauty in her culture. What impresses me more is her ability to use precisely what she had been apparently misusing to make a most poignant gesture to Jesus. She did not have to deny who she was; she didn't cover up her past. Her skills were redeemed in a great act of love. And Jesus realized it.

Interestingly, Jesus does not forgive her sins as such. He declares that because she is capable of such love, her sins must have already been forgiven her. Jesus' point is, of course, of some significance: there is a connection between being able to love and being forgiven. Jesus does declare that her sins are forgiven, but this would have been redundant if it is taken to be an actual act of forgiveness. Instead, it seems to be a confirmation of what has already occurred. Is this what often happens in the sacrament?

How to pray this passage

I would suggest that the first time through, you attend to the story as written. You might pay some attention to Jesus' own reactions: would he have been surprised by the woman? Embarrassed? After that, though, you might want to place yourself in the sinful woman's or Simon's position. An interesting way of praying this passage is to ask yourself where your greatest weakness is, and imagine a way to have that weakness turned into a gift for Jesus. It is often precisely in our weakness that Jesus has enough room to get through to us. Again, it is often in our weakness, even when it's mixed with real sinfulness, that we are perceived to be most effective in the apostolate.

In terms of ethics, a powerful point can be made. Much of our reluctance to take Jesus absolutely seriously is our fear that we would have to start over again from scratch, that following Jesus means a denial of our own history, a history of grace and sin combined. Because we cannot conceive of such a starting-over, we tend to refuse the possibility of changing our ways. Because we cannot start our country over again, dissolve all of our structures, we can quickly assume that these structures are irredeemable. But this passage suggests otherwise. Ethics is concerned with enacting possibilities, even creating new possibilities, but it is always focused on real possibilities. Belief in the power of grace, in the redeemability of creation, is precisely a belief that there is a way to get where we're going from here. Simon Peter remained Simon Peter, bumbling, saying the wrong thing at the wrong time. Paul did not try to deny his past after his conversion. And the woman in this passage still did what she knew best. What happened is their goals changed. There was a different logic at work. They embraced a new strategy for their lives. Something new became an imaginable possibility for them. And they pursued it.

The belief in the redeemability of our world is key. Redeemability is worked out in history, in the progressive steps we take in pursuit of the better possibility, as informed by our gospel-inspired imaginations of what the world could be. It means taking sin seriously, but not so seriously as to posit the domination of sin over God's grace. Hope insists that fidelity to God's strategy remains possible in our world – no matter how deeply enmeshed in sin we become: all things are possible for God.

Who do people say I am? (Luke 9.18–27; Mark 8.27–33)

This narrative, while interesting, is not at all easy to penetrate. Why did Jesus ask his disciples what people were saying about him? Why did he want to know? Why would it have mattered? One way of answering these questions is to suggest that Jesus was actually wondering who he was, that he was looking to his apostles for support.

This approach is not too far-fetched, for there is an important turn in the gospel here. At this point in his public career, Jesus is more than able to read the writing on the wall. He knows that he's going to be in for trouble. Hence, the first prophecy of the passion which occurs in the same story. Yet this must have troubled him: it could not have been what he had expected from the beginning. Most of us expect God to bless our work; we expect that when we place our trust in God, God will, in turn, protect us and draw fruit from our apostolic efforts. There is no reason to suspect that Jesus would have had different expectations. He had hoped and expected that the Kingdom would actually take root and bear fruit. He had not been preaching for nothing. Yet the opposition was growing. Could Jesus have been wondering whether he had made a wrong turn somewhere, overlooked some indication of God's will?

This is perhaps a bit clearer in Mark's version, for Mark included the famous episode where Peter tried to talk Jesus out of going to Jerusalem. The power of Jesus' retort, 'Get behind me Satan', suggests that Peter was indeed a tempter. It was as though Peter had inadvertently found Jesus' point of vulnerability; it was as though Jesus had said to Peter, 'If you only knew, Peter, just how much I've desired not to go to Jerusalem; if you only knew how sorely tempted I have been to run. If you only knew how foggy everything is right now. Peter, I needed your support; instead you tempted me: you kicked me when I was down!'

How to pray this passage

Luke opens the narrative with Jesus praying, suggesting that Jesus' question about his own identity arose from prayer itself.

You might spend some time with Jesus in his prayer, trying to feel his concern, in the midst of all this turmoil, to discern properly what God was requiring of him. You might try to taste his fear, for he is evidently struggling with the mounting persecution, struggling with having to go to Jerusalem to proclaim the Good News there. You might want to switch and use Mark's passage and try to get close to what Jesus might have felt when Peter tempted him. Can you appreciate just how tempted he must have been, how disappointed he must have been, how lonely he must have felt?

Jesus found himself in the same situation anyone who follows him finds him or herself in. Opposition is inevitable. Convincing people that they are unconditionally loved by God, that they are to love their enemies concretely in their lives – this sort of teaching upsets everything. As we have hinted, our world feeds off fear. We control people by fear. We sell things to people by engaging their fears – even if only the fear of being unhappy or out of step with everyone else. But those who believe in God's radical trustworthiness cannot be trusted to act like everyone else. They might try to change things. They might question time-honoured structures. Their more ultimate concerns might make them unreliable. They may be committed to something as arcane as *the good* rather than *the policy*. They might imperil a fragile national consensus; or worse, they may act without allegiance to the nation state, arguing in favour of some higher values.

Though these dangers seem ethereal, they are nonetheless real. There's a famous US document which was leaked to the public quite a few years ago. It identified liberation theology as a geopolitical threat and outlined an unashamedly conscious strategy of bankrolling and supporting conservative fundamentalist groups and conservative church leaders throughout Latin America. Their foe was not liberation theology as such, but the radical gospel, a gospel which foments hope, which encourages action, which reveals possibilities for change. The hundreds of thousands of Latin American martyrs were (and continue to be) killed for the same reasons that Jesus himself was killed: he was a real threat. His simple message about God's love had to be suppressed.

The Transfiguration (Luke 9.28–36)

Luke recounts that this event also occurred while Jesus was praying. That is important, for one of the mistakes we can make in approaching this important event is to turn it into an amazing scene fit for an epic movie. But Luke presents it as a religious experience once again, and this shouldn't be dismissed too easily. More than that though, we can often take the Transfiguration completely out of context and thereby lose sight of what this might have meant for Jesus and his apostles.

If Jesus was indeed struggling with his vocation, wondering perhaps whether he had taken a wrong turn somewhere, if he was beset by internal doubts about whether to go to Jerusalem, then this event is crucial to an understanding of Jesus' choice. Jesus' going to Jerusalem and his willingness to undergo suffering as the cost of his fidelity were clearly the matters at hand. Jesus' fears were being addressed very directly. And in this light, it is no accident that the words from the clouds are almost identical to the words Jesus heard at his Baptism, for the Transfiguration is a clear confirmation of Jesus' initial vocation experience, as if God were saying to Jesus, 'You have indeed chosen correctly. Go to Jerusalem. You will suffer, but trust me, you are still on the right track. I am still pleased with you. You are still and will forever be my Beloved Son.' Recognizing that Jesus is now a member of a small faith community, the words, which were originally addressed only to Jesus at the Baptism, are now addressed to the apostles who accompanied him in prayer as well.

I think we can presume that this event happened because it had to happen. Jesus needed to be confirmed at this point in his career. He needed to hear God speak in the depths of his being once again, otherwise he would not have made it to Jerusalem. The doubts would have caught up with him.

How to pray this passage

Again, it's important, I would think, to get close to Jesus' own experience, to be with him in prayer, to let his doubts and worries touch us at the deepest level of our being. His prayer would have been tough prayer, soul-searching, excruciating. He might well have been feeling very alone, perhaps even abandoned: maybe that's why he had invited some of the apostles to be with him. Feeling all that with Jesus, we can better appreciate how welcome this epiphany of God actually was, how much Jesus needed to hear his Father, how much he needed to hear God confirm his choice, his strategy, his identity. You might even ask for a similar confirmation in your own life; or you might recall instances when God has confirmed you; or you might be called to trust that God does and will confirm us when we need such confirmation.

Of course, Jesus was right to wonder whether he had gone wrong somewhere. While we should expect opposition, we should not naively take opposition to be a sure sign of our being on the right track. What is important, however, is to do as Jesus did: namely, to live a life of prayer, a life of intimacy with God, fully expecting to hear again and again God's words, 'I love you. Trust me.' Jesus had every reason to doubt whether God was indeed loving him. This wasn't a lack of faith, instead it was a real question. And God addressed the question. We should expect nothing less in our own lives, as long as we are attentive to God. We ought, however, to be wary of thinking that a single conversion experience suffices to ground hope. It clearly wasn't at all sufficient for Jesus.

One of the more significant things about Luke's portrayal of Jesus is Jesus' penchant for prayer. We don't get the sense that Jesus prayed at a set time, but he was rigorous in his prayer life. Rather, we see a man who brought all of his significant decisions to prayer before acting. Actually, if you were to go through Luke's gospel, you can easily detect this pattern of prayer first, then a significant decision – whether it was choosing the apostles, or confronting his adversaries. It is a lesson very much apropos to ethics, for without a life of prayer, it is very unlikely that a long-term commitment to pursuing the good can be sustained: the temptation to avoid suffering is just too strong for us unless we are consciously in relation to God.

Setting his jaw for Jerusalem (Luke 9.51)

Though it's only one line in Scripture, the words 'And Jesus set his jaw for Jerusalem' have always captivated Christians. The phrase sets the context for the rest of Jesus' life. At this point, he actually chooses. He has had his doubts. God has confirmed him. He has reached out to his apostles – at least they're still with him. He's fully cognizant of the need to go to Jerusalem, for he's convinced, as he said, that it would not be right for a prophet to die outside of Jerusalem. If he hadn't gone to Jerusalem, he would have had to spend the rest of his life running away from Jerusalem. If he hadn't been willing to face the music, as it were, who would have believed him any longer? Without credibility he would have let down his apostles terribly. In fact, avoiding Jerusalem would have meant giving it all up: the dream of the Kingdom, the Good News of God's trustworthiness, the proclamation that we have nothing to lose by obeying God, the wonderful appreciation that the persecuted are strangely blessed, that love of enemy might build up the Kingdom more than violence. He would have been bowing to the power of evil, accepting its dominion.

But he could not give it all up; he would not let his friends down; he still believed in God's strategy, God's way; and so he set his jaw against all his surface inclinations in the direction of his deepest desire, in the direction of his religion's most powerful religious symbol, but in a direction which represented at the same time his deepest dread: Jerusalem.

How to pray this passage

I think this little line can be a very poignant focal point for appreciating that Jesus really did struggle to be faithful, even after his experience on the mountain. It is an opportunity to be with Jesus as he decides in favour of going to Jerusalem, an invitation to feel the strange appropriateness of his choice. You might also sit with the seeming inevitability (and the gospels are quite clear on this) of his suffering: no one can say what Jesus said and do what Jesus did without creating powerful opposition. It's as though Jesus suffered quite particularly because of the way he lived. This is the strangely satisfying and logical outcome of his life. We could do worse than simply be with Jesus as he does what he must do.

Jesus had to set his jaw for Jerusalem. He had to choose. He had to make a difficult choice. And it remained difficult despite his closeness to God. Many of us have different expectations.

Many of us want God to possess us, to make the good so attractive that we will not have to choose at all: we want to let ourselves be pulled by God, pulled by the good. We don't want to choose. But God won't possess.

Doing the good costs. Doing the good may mean sacrificing my own life, or it may mean sacrificing *our* lives, for the gospel is addressed not to individuals, but to communities. Many of us understand the need to sacrifice our own lives, but we stop short of thinking that the good might cost even more than that. We fail to appreciate that Jesus knew only too well that his disciples were likely to meet the same fate as he was going to meet. They too would have to set their jaws. Many of us are shy to speak this clearly. We are wary of asking others to do *the hard but good thing*. But the fact of the matter is that the Gospel strategy is a communal strategy. If we all were to love our enemies, new possibilities would emerge. The Gospel does not call us to sacrifice for its own sake, but for the sake of a good – something worth sacrificing *for*. And the sacrifice makes no sense unless the good sought is reachable. But that takes real community.

Providence (Luke 12.4–7; 22–34)

Once again, there is some danger that we will take Jesus' lovely teachings on providence out of context and thereby misunderstand them completely. Here, Jesus speaks of God's loving care in words we know so well, speaking of sparrows and ravens; the hairs on our head having been counted by God; the lilies and the grass; about there being no need for anxiety, for concern over food and clothes. The danger is that we will take this in a naïve sense, in an optimistic sense. But if Luke has placed this passage even close to being chronologically correct, we should know by now that Jesus had few illusions about the persecution besetting him as he travelled and preached. Though Jesus clearly expected God to pull him through and to vindicate him in the end, he nowhere suggested that God would make everything easy for him. He had probably already seen what had happened to John the Baptist, and so it was only too evident that divine providence did not save John from suffering or death. Moreover, Jesus was too close to the suffering people, too compassionate to overlook the very real depths of their poverty and misery. No; Jesus is not saying that everything's going to be absolutely lovely, that if we trust God, God will guard and guide us physically. Instead, Jesus is suggesting that God remains absolutely trustworthy, even when it's not obvious: and this is true even in the midst of his own suffering, on the way to Jerusalem.

The power of Jesus' belief in providence is infinitely more forceful when appreciated in terms of his own experience and struggles. This was not an easy teaching to give under these or any other circumstances, and, if you read on a bit, the context of struggle and opposition is clearly stated in the gospel.

How to pray this passage

I would ask God to reveal this trustworthiness to me, to see it, to know it, to feel it, as Jesus did. I'd ask to know this in my heart of hearts, and to see how it pulsates at the very core of the gospel, how it makes the other teachings that much clearer: God is trustworthy, ultimately we have nothing to lose, so we can dare to love God and neighbour without reserve.

One of the dangers of religious people doing ethical reflection is precisely this naïve sense of providence. Though it can lead to a certain recklessness, it can also lead to a debilitating desperation as cherished notions of providence fail to match up to the reality of suffering in our world. The challenge of this passage is hardly to believe that God is so trustworthy that everything is going to be roses – that is optimism, not faith. The challenge is to believe God to be absolutely trustworthy even when everything is going wrong – that is faith. But even that is not the full story, for the enduring challenge is to remain faithful to God's strategy, to know that the worst of life's blows do not constitute the final chapter. The resurrection of Jesus by the Father is God's clear message that Jesus had indeed discerned God's strategy correctly. That message was clearly meant for us.

The heart of Jesus (Luke 13.31–5; Luke 19.41–7)

I find these passages, Jesus' lament for Jerusalem in Luke 13.31–5 and the later lament in Luke 19.21 where Jesus wept for Jerusalem, to be among the more powerful in the gospels. They both reveal the depth of Jesus' love, the passion with which he experienced life and people. Few of us have ever wept over a city.

Key to appreciating these few lines is situating them within the journey to Jerusalem. At a time when he might have been expected to hate Jerusalem, Jesus instead recalls how often he had wanted to embrace the city, and does so by using a very compelling and lovely, indeed a very feminine, image. Yet he is not blinded by his love; he realizes the obdurate and serious nature of Jerusalem's choice. There is nothing sugar-coated about this love.

The second text includes Luke's account of Jesus' cleansing of the temple. In John's gospel, John places this event at the very beginning of his gospel, suggesting that this was the cause of a large part of the opposition to Jesus. In Luke's gospel, the incident occurred as soon as Jesus entered Jerusalem, and the opposition was already strong before then. Nonetheless, the incident communicates very effectively the powerful feelings that Jesus must have had at that point in his life.

Some people use the cleansing incident to countenance the use of violence. They read into the story, choosing to imagine Jesus as whipping people, even though this is not mentioned anywhere. (Animal rights people would not be appeased, for he probably used the whips to drive out the animals, though again, it is the noise – the sonic boom actually – of a whip, more than its touch, that scares animals.) It is important to read on in Luke and to notice that, right after the cleansing, Luke says that Jesus taught in the temple every day and that people clung to his words – hardly the reaction expected had Jesus in fact used violence against people. Still the passage points to what is called *righteous anger*, and it is an important corrective to popular views of the ideal Christian being a thoroughly pacific, unperturbable sort.

How to pray this passage

I pray these passages quite simply by seeing these episodes as revealing Jesus' heart, his deepest desires. I try to be with Jesus in the pain and the anger. I also take them as a challenge. Luke says that Jesus shed tears over Jerusalem, saying 'If you in your turn had only understood on this day the message of peace. But, alas, it is hidden from your eyes . . . And all because you didn't recognize your opportunity when God offered it!' (Luke 19.41–4) I wonder to myself why I don't shed tears over my cities, over my world. Obviously, Jesus wasn't simply feeling sorry for himself: he was deeply hurt because they were destroying themselves. They refused to hear this message of peace, and their refusal would inevitably destroy them.

What Jesus was experiencing was the gap between what could be and what was. The gap is the space of suffering. Refusing to act to bridge the gap entails, not the sort of redemptive suffering that Jesus was to go through, but the destructive suffering due to our repeatedly choosing death over life, evil over good. And Jesus had the courage to experience this suffering; he felt its destructiveness; he was vulnerable enough to let it hurt him to the point of tears.

Like Jesus, we must have strategies of vulnerability. We must feel the destructiveness of our world precisely as destructiveness. Without being open to the suffering, we don't hear suffering's complaint – a first glimpse of hope that someone is looking for new possibilities. Without knowing that destructiveness, the urgency to close the gap between possibility and actuality fails to impress itself upon us. Hence the need for solidarity with society's victims. If we cannot cry over cities, how united are we to Jesus?

Render unto Caesar (Luke 20.19–26)

This passage has been used to justify the most horrendous crimes against God and humanity – all because of some all-too-convenient readings which twist what seem to many of us to have been Jesus' original meaning. The worst of the wrong interpretations sees the existence of two good laws: one divine and another human, each having some claim on us, requiring us to steer a course between them. A more adequate interpretation can be had by simply reading the text out loud, placing a solemn emphasis on 'And to God, the things that are God's'. This suggests a further question, 'And what does not belong to God?' The answer is, of course, obvious, and the question is really rhetorical.

It does not seem as though Jesus was suggesting that God is not concerned with temporal affairs, for that was one of the primary emphases of his teaching: after all, Jesus had been at pains to emphasize that we should see our temporal lives as very much tied to love of God, that love of neighbour – especially of the poor, the oppressed, the enemy – is the actual measure of our love of God. Jesus was indeed suggesting that there are two discrete kingdoms, two competing strategies, but he had expected us to choose between the two, not chart a convenient course between them. Yet that is precisely what we have done.

We read that the people marvelled at his answer. In effect, Jesus' answer silenced his interlocutors; and it did so because it suggested that they had asked the wrong question: they had asked whether they should pay taxes to Caesar, but Jesus suggested they should have asked what they should give to God.

How to pray this passage

If you're one of those who have been misled by a 'convenient' reading of this text, you might want to let Jesus' own words challenge you. You might let Jesus' idea that you have to choose between the kingdoms lead you to a real choice yourself. For instance, you might believe in capital punishment, arguing that, even though Jesus forbade revenge and violence, urging forgiveness at all times, the secular state has the right to use violence because they come under a different law than the one Jesus proclaimed. Let Jesus ask you whether you haven't truncated God's sovereignty over all aspects of life.

Though this is not easy 'stuff' to pray on, you might want to let the radicalness of Jesus' teachings take hold of you, let it really challenge you, challenge all your beliefs and all your opinions of everything. At least for a few minutes. Our world has missed the point of the teaching entirely; and it would be surprising were we to have escaped the world's influence entirely. Don't we in fact separate our religious from our secular lives? Aren't there areas in our lives – personal lives and collective lives – where we are hard-pressed to figure out how God matters at all?

The Last Supper (Luke 22.14–38)

The first challenge is to understand what actually went on that evening, what Jesus himself had intended. Only then can any theological meaning be usefully applied to the event and to our repetition of that event. Unfortunately, most of us received a theology of the Eucharist prior to our really understanding Jesus' intentions.

In a nutshell, Jesus' desire was to remain united to his disciples through his suffering and death. He asked them to repeat this event in his memory because of his very human desire to have them remember him. It would be anachronistic, i.e. playing havoc with time, to suggest that Jesus intended to set up a sacrament, per se. The original meaning of the Eucharist is to be found in Jesus' heart, in Jesus' eyes, in Jesus' intentions. Moreover, such an approach can remind us that it is not our desire to be united to Jesus that is crucial, but his desire and prayer to be united with us.

Consider the following:

As he faced his death, Jesus took a loaf of bread and gave thanks in a way he had never quite done before. He broke the bread and, staring into his disciples' eyes, offered it to them, as if to say,

This is my body; this is my life; this is everything I have taught you – my vision of the Kingdom, my love of our Father, my love for each of you. This is my very body.

Will you continue to be my disciples? My friends? Will you follow me through everything? Will you eat this with me? Will you remember me, this moment, for ever – by repeating this?

When supper ended, he repeated his invitation – even more clearly. He took a single cup and gave thanks once again. He looked at his friends, as if to say,

> This is my blood, my very spirit; this is all I have ever desired, all I have ever loved. This is the cup of my life which I am freely giving up in trust of my Father; and I offer it to you, my friends. This will be our covenant, the new covenant of discipleship.

> Will you share my life? Will you continue to follow me? Will you always call yourselves my friends? Will you drink this cup with me? Will you unite yourself to me for ever?

Then Jesus passed the cup and each disciple in turn drank from that same cup.

How to pray this passage

The most obvious way to pray this passage is to participate in the Eucharist, to be quite consciously aware that at communion time you are being invited to embrace, to say 'yes' to, Jesus' whole life: all his teachings, his hopes, his vision, his longings, his desires, his loves, his concerns, his vocation – and all this in response to his invitation to follow him as a disciple. To do this, most of us need to have prayed on the Last Supper using our imaginations at some point or other. We need to know intimately the depths of Jesus' love for his disciples, the longing he had to celebrate this last meal with them, and praying with Scripture is a perfect invitation to do so.

There is a sense, too, in which the Last Supper symbolizes much of Jesus' teaching. The meal was one of Jesus' most consistent images of the Kingdom. It symbolized for him the necessary communal nature of our living under God's reign. Jesus' own dining habits scandalized many. He seems not to have refused many invitations – not even from people who could hardly have been counted as sympathetic to his teaching. So, not only is our participation in the Eucharist an opening up of ourselves to Jesus' desire to be united to us, it can also be a tacit commitment to overcome all the barriers that separate us one from the other.

The Agony and Crucifixion (Luke 23.26–48)

Again, the narrative is familiar, so there is no need to expand on that. However, there is a theological problem which often prevents people from truly understanding the crucifixion. The problem is that many of us believe that God wanted Jesus to die, that somehow this pleased God, that God wanted Jesus to die to 'pay' for our sins, that God sacrificed his only son to correct an imbalance somewhere. This creates a monster out of God. It creates a God who demands blood sacrifices, who actually plans the murder of his Son to appease his anger. If we know anything from Jesus' preaching, we should know that this does not resemble the God Jesus revealed in any way whatsoever. And yet many of us have laboured under this misconception for decades.

Jesus died because his enemies killed him. Not because God arranged things so that Judas would betray Jesus. Not because this was the way it had to be to fulfil the prophecies. No, Jesus died because he was murdered, and he was murdered because he was perceived – quite correctly, mind you – to be a threat to the established order.

But what, some may ask, about all the texts that suggest that this was God's will? Clearly, it was God's will that Jesus go to Jerusalem, but it would have been God's preference that Jerusalem convert and embrace Jesus' message. Yet I presume that God, and I am certain that Jesus also, realized that there was little likelihood of that, and Jesus discerned that God was requiring him to go to Jerusalem nonetheless. Why? To appease God? Or was it more likely because God desired Jesus' integrity, because God saw what Jesus saw, namely that it would not have been right to die outside Jerusalem, that Jesus really did have to go to the very centre of Jewish life and proclaim his Good News there, even at the risk of losing his life.

We can say for certain that God wanted Jesus to be faithful no matter the cost. And as much as God might have wanted Jesus to live, still God did not want Jesus to live by compromise. In this sense, God wanted Jesus to go to Jerusalem, not because Jesus' death would please him but because faithfulness was the very essence of Jesus' life and mission, and fidelity was worth more than this life. It still is. Simply put, Jesus reluctantly died because there was no other way to remain faithful, and God blessed that decision.

How to pray this passage

St Paul and numerous Christians since have stressed that Jesus suffered for my sins, for me, as if to say that his death was not simply an act of political defiance, an unfortunate example of what happens to good people throughout the world. The Gospel writers were at pains to stress that Jesus actually chose to die, and not for any abstract principle. He certainly could have run away, but he chose not to. He actually chose to die for all his followers (and thus in a real sense for me, even though he didn't know me), out of loyalty to his Father and to his disciples. He could have taken Peter's advice and not gone to Jerusalem, but he would thereby have undone everything he had preached, everything he had taught. As we said above, had he turned, he would have had to spend the rest of his life running away from Jerusalem. He chose to go to Jerusalem, because in a profound sense he had to go to Jerusalem. He would have destroyed his disciples had he not done so, even though they didn't want him to go. He went for God's sake, for his own sake, and for the sake of his disciples, for the sake of his teachings. Without at least some appreciation of the utterly interpersonal nature of Jesus' death and the central element of Jesus' own decision, the Passion can only be seen as an obscene and revolting event.

The greatest challenge to praying on the Crucifixion is to remain present to Jesus in his suffering. It's not at all easy, but that shouldn't surprise us. Only a consummate sadist could find any enjoyment in that experience. In fact, the apostles remain prime examples of just how difficult it must have been, and how demanding it still is, to stay with Jesus through his Passion. Staying quietly with Jesus at the foot of the cross is an extraordinary labour of love which requires 'great effort', and we may even have to 'force ourselves' out of love to feel what we want to feel. The choice must be deliberate enough to overcome the revulsion which we feel at the violent suffering of someone we love.

Many people who pray on the Passion want to feel profound movements of sadness, but I'm not sure that we should ask to feel great pain and suffering because we feel bad about Jesus' Passion. Rather, we ask for these 'gifts' primarily because we want to share Jesus' experience. What is called for is com-passion – feeling with Jesus, rather than for Jesus: we are not called to our own suffering in prayer but to radical union with Jesus even in his suffering. This is rather crucial. All too often we respond to

Jesus the way we would react were we to witness a horrible accident: we turn inward, we're super-conscious of ourselves and of our feelings. Instead, it would be better to be present to Jesus himself in his Passion.

Jesus' Passion convinces us that suffering can be expressive of love. Clearly, no suffering is a value, but suffering, like everything else, can be redeemed by God: it can be turned to the good. Those who are seriously considering following Jesus will have to come to grips with what it means to be a *suffering servant*; they will have to go through a purification of their desires, coming face-to-face with fear and selfishness. In a way unlike any other Christian symbol, the cross represents the victory of love over self-interest. We see how naïve understandings of providence must fail. We see the ultimate cost of saying no to the original three temptations in the wilderness. Hence the words in the Gospel that the tempter would return at 'the appointed time' (Luke 4.13). We see what our world does to those who eschew self-fulfilment, power, and prestige. We see how far a person can go in trusting God.

The Resurrection (Luke 24)

He is risen! Jesus Christ is risen, but you wouldn't know it half the time. One of the standard ways of reacting to Jesus' resurrection is to say, 'Great. We're going to be raised too.'

Since almost the very beginning, many of us have taken the experience of the Risen Jesus, of God's response to the life of Jesus, and universalized it, we've made it apply to everyone. But there's a problem with this. The problem is not the universalization, for that is true, but it is that we universalize far too quickly. We jump to theology before we realize just what actually went on. We try to bring ourselves, all of humanity, into the picture before we clearly see the key players: Jesus and God. The first thing to say about the resurrection is that God raised Jesus from the dead. The second thing to say is that God raised Jesus from the dead because of the life Jesus lived, because Jesus remained faithful. Jesus was not simply a classroom prop at a divine lecture about the universal resurrection. Hardly, for in the resurrection, God quite specifically revealed that Jesus' life met with divine approval, that a life lived out of radical trust in God is not spurned by God.

Jesus' life, death and resurrection belong together. Salvation is not just dying and rising with Jesus: it is *living* and dying and rising with him who has the words of eternal life. They belong together. The resurrection reveals to us that our response to God's absolute trustworthiness is to follow Jesus, to follow his strategy concretely, to believe that Jesus meant what he said, to know in our heart of hearts that Jesus' strategy works – because it has already worked inasmuch as God has corroborated Jesus' faith.

Belief in the resurrection, far from pointing us away from this life, is an affirmation that the Kingdom is within reach, it has broken into this life. It cannot be postponed: the treasure is found, the fish are caught, the light is on, the seed is sown and the harvest in, the yeast well-kneaded, the pearl has been bought, the salt has flavour to spare, the banquet is ready, the unwise maidens late. God's strategy has been revealed. Nothing more needs to be added.

In the resurrection God has played the divine hand; and God was found to be worthy of trust. Ultimately, there is nothing to be afraid of. Now we can love our enemies; we can work for peace; we can share our wealth; we can take our nuclear swords and hammer them into sickles, and food, and education, and health. There's nothing to be afraid of. Jesus said so, and God agreed.

Belief in the resurrection is our agreeing with God's judgement on Jesus' life. It is our saying 'yes' to Jesus' whole life. It is our acceptance of our responsibility to be disciples of that same Jesus, to be harbingers of his Good News. Jesus has not just come back to life; but, in a way that defies description, he has come back to this life, and in so doing he is decidedly carrying the specifics of his historical life with him for ever. Belief in the resurrection then, is a commitment to Jesus, to his history, to the whole of his life, and to a concrete discipleship which takes him and his message absolutely seriously.

How to pray this passage

Jesus must have enjoyed being raised. In praying on the appearance accounts, it would be important to attend to Jesus' own joy, his own gratitude to God. It would be important to take his greeting 'Do not be afraid' seriously, seeing it, not simply as a response to his unlikely presence, but also a pointing of the way for the future.

Most of the appearance accounts are ambiguous at best. Mary did not recognize Jesus; neither did several of his disciples on the road to Emmaus; neither did Peter by the Sea of Tiberius. It seems that the evangelists are trying to tell us two things at once: first, that Jesus' appearances were not normal events, that they were faith-experiences, that, without faith, you could have missed the whole thing; and second, that these experiences were nonetheless real. The latter point is stressed in such things as Jesus' eating, Thomas' touching of Jesus' wounds, and so on.

Some people want to argue that the resurrection was an historical event, but the evangelists seem to be at pains to convince us that these experiences were more *real than* any historical event. The evangelists could not explain the resurrection: they didn't even try. Instead, they spoke of powerful experiences of the risen Jesus, of how lives were radically changed, of how fearful disciples were turned into bold leaders, of how a church was born.

The lack of explanation, the lack of unambiguous description – these factors might upset some. However, there is something supremely important to notice: namely, that the faith-filled nature of the experience of the risen Jesus means that our experiences of Jesus today (for he is still risen) are potentially similar to the experiences his earliest disciples had. Indeed, the apostles' willingness to admit St Paul into the ranks of apostles was based on an experience which can only be described as Paul's powerful *religious* experience of Jesus. As far as they were concerned, this was not unlike their own previous experience.

With regard to ethics, there is no ethics without hope. It is important that our hope be based, not simply on a lucky-but-blind guess that God is trustworthy, but on the concrete actions of a trustworthy God. We need to experience the resurrected Jesus, else we have not allowed God to speak the ultimate word of hopefulness.

The Gospel of Luke and Social Ethics, Montreal: Ignatian Publications, 1988.

6

Spirituality and the Trinity

This last chapter is an extract from an incomplete Local Non-Stipendiary Ministry Training Course for both laity and clergy for the Diocese of Salisbury whilst JPC was himself a Non-Stipendiary Minister, before he left to become Principal of St Chad's College, University of Durham. The focus of the course was to explore the fundamental doctrines of the Nicene Creed.

Beginnings

The beginning of Christian faith is the Spirit-authored experience of those early Christians who knew Jesus best. These early Christians had a powerful experience of the Risen Lord; and in the light of that experience, they recalled the life of Jesus: what he said, what he did, how he lived, how he died. Right from the start, they began to do something we call theology: they reflected on their experience in an attempt to discover its significance. In other words, in trying to understand their experience, they interpreted their experience. Some interpretations were wild, others had the ring of authenticity. People wrote down some of their recollections, stories, legends, as well as the letters that went back and forth, trying to explore the significance of Jesus in the communal lives of his followers. As time went on, questions about the authority of these writings had to be answered, and decisions were made. These decisions enshrined certain interpretations, certain stories, certain letters, recognizing them as part of new Scripture. But these Scriptures raised as many questions as they answered. Squabbles broke out, especially about such things as the divinity and humanity of Jesus, the divine personhood of the Holy Spirit, and their relationship to the Father. The resulting Christian creeds enshrine decisions about various ways of understanding God, attempting to hold all of Scripture together.

Belief in one God

Belief in the Trinity is perhaps the most distinctive of all Christian beliefs. Belief in the Trinity is not a belief in three gods, nor is it a belief in one super-god and two subsidiary gods. It is not a belief in one God who is revealed in three forms or modes. Rather our trinitarian belief is the belief that three divine persons are so united to one another that they are actually and inseparably one God, one Supreme Being. The union is utterly complete, so much so that there is only one divine will in God. As complicated as the language is, it should still be vaguely familiar. But sometimes such theological language is so familiar that we do not realize the full significance of what we are saying. To use other ways of speaking, belief in the Trinity means believing that our ultimate reality is communitarian: after all, the Trinity is a community of three divine persons. Belief in the Trinity means that what really matters in life – in the universe – is relationships: after all, the Trinity is a series of relationships among three divine persons. Belief in the Trinity means believing that there is something fundamental in life about being distinct and yet being united at the same time (i.e. loving), just as the persons of the Trinity are unique and united.

But what would make you believe in the Trinity? Because it is a good idea? Because millions of people have believed in it before you? Or because you yourself have experienced the Trinity? Does it not make more sense to expect to find something of the Trinity in our experience, something that allows us to say that our belief in the Trinity is our response to the Trinity revealing itself to us, something that allows us to say that God is ultimately the one who is responsible for our believing in a Trinity of divine persons?

Experience the Trinity: the One

So what would an experience of the Trinity be like? There can be no single answer, for God reveals God's self to us in many ways. It is tempting to say that we can experience God the Father, then we can experience Jesus, and finally we can experience the Spirit, and because we experience these three divine 'persons' we believe in a Trinity. But that accounts for belief in the Three, not for belief in the One. What could possibly justify our experience of the Trinity as one God? One answer (and it is the one suggested here) is that to experience the Trinity is to experience the three divine persons loving one another. In other words, the Christian experience of the Trinity is an experience of the inner workings of the Trinity, it is a tasting of the divine love and the divine life that draw the three persons into infinite closeness; it is an experience of each divine person's desire for the other divine persons – desires so powerful, so pure, so all-consuming that the desires are gloriously fulfilled in a wonderous and unique unity: this justifies our saying that 'we believe in one God'.

Explained that way, we can perhaps begin to imagine how the early Church might first have experienced and subsequently realized that Jesus and the Father were not just one but one in being.

Though we cannot recreate past experiences, it is nonetheless possible to understand how such early experiences of Jesus' unity with the Father could have been embraced and eventually clarified in the language of the creeds. Similarly, we can understand how the Church could build on the Pauline image of the Spirit groaning within each of us, groaning for the Father and the Son (Rom. 8.26), and drawing us into that holy union of three divine persons.

Experience the Trinity: the Three

Now all of that is to look at how the three become one, but what of the one becoming three? An equally authentic way of experiencing the Trinity is to experience God as being so creative, so dynamic, so bursting with love, that God could not possibly be only one person. There is something almost necessary about the Trinity: not necessary in the sense of there being some law or rule book that tells God how to be God, but in the sense that such a divine being could not possibly be alone.

Indeed, the language of the creeds suggests that the second person of the Trinity, Jesus Christ, is being constantly begotten of the Father from all ages. He was never created out of nothing. Instead, there is something so creative about God that God is constantly becoming three, just as there is something so loving about God that God is constantly becoming one.

This, then, is the challenge: to ask ourselves whether we believe in the Trinity, to ask ourselves why we believe in the Trinity. And if we are humble enough to admit that we might not have had the kind of religious experience that leads to faith in the Trinity, let us be thankful that we can detect God tilling the soil of our hearts and making us spiritually hungry for just such an experience. Christians are entirely justified in praying their hearts out for the grace of an experience of the Most Holy Trinity.

Trinity as mystery

Trying to understand the Trinity is one of the hardest things in the world to do. After all, and despite what has just been said, we formally define the Trinity as a mystery: how can there be three persons and still only one God, one Being? The best theological answer we can give is that it is beyond all explanation. Even when we get to heaven, the Trinity will still be a mystery. It will still be a mystery because the Trinity cannot be explained in terms of anything else. It is the highest truth, and it cannot be broken down into little bits. Understanding the Trinity is not like trying to understand an automobile engine: engines may be mysteries to some people, but engines are understandable, if you have the right information.

The Trinity is different: it is not because we lack information that we do not understand the Trinity, it is because God is beyond all understanding, because God is the very source of everything. The Trinity is the ultimate truth – that is why we cannot understand it: we cannot explain it in terms of other things, we cannot break it down to little bits.

Some may ask, if we shall not understand the Trinity even in heaven, what is the point? What is the point of believing something that we do not understand? Is God so much beyond us that we shall never get to know the Trinity?

Experience of the Trinity

The answer is that we shall not know the Trinity from the outside: whatever heaven is, it is probably not some big information centre where all of a sudden, we are tied into the biggest computer, suddenly knowing everything. No, from the little we know about heaven, the afterlife is about being perfectly united with

God. We shall not know the Trinity the way we know anything else. Instead, we shall be perfectly united to the Trinity: each of us and all of us together will become part of the mystery of the Trinity itself, and we shall become part of the very life of the Trinity. We shall not understand the Trinity; instead, we shall experience the Trinity first-hand.

Now, this is not too surprising. Understanding something or someone means reducing that something or someone. Few married people would say that they fully understand their partner or loved one. Few children would pretend fully to understand their parents. The other person remains something of a mystery. There is something in the other person that is simply too wonderful to put into words. Could anyone say to someone, I've solved my wife, or I've solved my husband? It is the same with the Trinity: the Trinity is not a problem to be solved; it is not a puzzle; you understand the Trinity not by figuring it out, but by experiencing the Trinity. By being loved by and by falling in love with the source of all life and all love.

The key is to realize that what is most important is not knowing lots about God. Faith is not just information. It is not just concerned with saying the right words. It is not just about getting theological answers right. Faith is really about being grasped by God. Faith is not about explaining the Trinity, but about experiencing the Trinity. Faith is having been touched by a Being who is beyond all explanation, who tugs at our hearts, and who will never let us go.

Trinitarian prayer

So, how do we experience this Trinity? There is no blueprint, because such experiences are always gifts: we cannot cause them. What do we do? Well, as Christians, we pray. We are urged to pray constantly. And if we want to experience God, if we want to know the Trinity from the inside, we shall have to pray. The Trinity is not just an idea, not a problem to be solved. We have to allow the Trinity of Divine Persons a chance to reveal themselves to us.

In prayer, we have to let go, we have to let God be God, we have to stop trying to grab God and instead let God grab us; we have to let go our ideas about God, so that we can experience God – not our ideas. Ideas are important, but God's revelation is more important. And if we do that, if we say to God, 'Come and find me,' God tends to honour our request, and God reveals the Trinity; somehow or other, sooner or later, God gives us an experience of God's mystery. And we know it when it happens, because we feel ourselves drawn out of ourselves, we feel a kind of lightness, we begin spontaneously to praise, we find ourselves saying thank you. It may be very quiet, or it may be powerful. Whatever happens, we shall not have any more information about the Trinity than we had before. Instead, we shall begin to adore the Trinity and in adoring the most Glorious Trinity, the mystery actually increases! But the mystery of the Trinity is no longer a puzzle: it becomes wondrous, full of life; it becomes too grand to be contained in ideas. The mystery, far from being a problem, is an absolute joy. And even the mystics, whom many believe had a more-or-less direct experience of God, tell us that their experiences lasted barely a second, if that: the glory and wonder of the Trinity is almost too much to handle. Moses thought that you would actually die if you saw God face-to-face.

This is not to say that the only way to experience the mystery of the Trinity is in prayer; but it is true that in Christian tradition, and in Jesus' own life, such experiences tend to happen during prayer: think of Jesus' baptism and transfiguration. If you read the texts in Luke's gospel carefully, those experiences happened when Jesus was praying.

So if we really want to plumb the depths of the doctrine of the Trinity, we must be willing to pray, we must be willing to learn to pray. We have to let go and let God be God, we have to let God reveal God's innermost self to us. We have to open ourselves to mystery, to let the full force of the mystery reveal itself to us. Then when we recite the Nicene Creed, when we say that we believe in one God, in three persons, we shall know whom we are believing in. We may not have any more information, but we shall actually know the Trinity as the glorious mystery that it is.

Praying the Trinity

Commit yourself to finding at least 20 minutes to pray in solitude and quiet a few times a week. Before beginning your prayer, find yourself a copy of the Gloria (communion booklets will do!).

Spend a few minutes getting comfortable and settle yourself down. Put aside any worries or concerns: you'll have plenty of time to resume worrying after your prayer, but during your prayer you are going to try to keep your mind and heart focused on God. Consciously and deliberately call upon the Holy Spirit, asking God to bless you during this period of prayer. Repeat this request until you can honestly say that you do really desire to experience God.

Then slowly read through the words of the Gloria. Ask the Holy Spirit to animate your prayer, and ask Jesus to pray with you. Ask to join Jesus in his praise of the Father. Then pray the Gloria a few times very slowly. If you get to the point where you feel that you're in a state of praise, don't use any more words, just let your entire being praise God, Father, Son, and Holy Spirit. Allow a few minutes of silence at the end of the prayer to simply let yourself be with God. Close with the Lord's Prayer.

I beg the Lord for an intimate knowledge of Jesus, that I might know him better, love him more deeply, and follow him ever more closely for the rest of my life.

Further Reading

Joseph P. Cassidy: Selected Publications A

Scripture and Christian Theology, Montreal: Concordia University, 1986.

History of Spirituality, Montreal: Concordia University, 1986.

An Introduction to Ignatian Prayer, Montreal: Ignatian Publications, 1988. Reprinted as *Praying the Gospels. An Introduction to Discipleship*, Montreal: Ignatian Spirituality Centre, 2003.

The Gospel of Luke and Social Ethics, Montreal: Ignatian Publications, 1988.

Joseph P. Cassidy: Selected Publications B

Pp. 37–4 in *Steps Towards Visible Unity*, Diocese of Durham; Churches together in Gainford: Second Roman-Catholic International Commission, 1999.

'Living Sacrifice' in Conway, S. (ed.), *Living the Eucharist*, London: Darton, Longman & Todd, 2001, pp. 1–12.

'Communal Discernment in a Christian College', *Borderlands: A Journal of Theology and Education*, 3 (2004), pp. 13–16.

'Anglican authority', *Foundation*, 2.1 (2005), pp. 1–14.

'An Introduction to Bernard Lonergan', *Foundation* 3.1 (2006), pp. 1–17.

'Who's in. Who's out' in M. D. Chapman (ed.), *Living the Magnificat*, London: Mowbray/Continuum, 2007, pp. 103–9.

'On Discernment' in R. C. Macswain and M. Ward (eds), *The Cambridge Companion to C. S. Lewis*, Cambridge: Cambridge University Press, 2010, pp. 132–45.

'Radical Anglicanism' in M. D. Chapman (ed.), *The Hope of Things to Come: Anglicanism and the future*, London: Mowbray/Continuum (2010), pp. 88–101.

For further references and information see Ann Loades, 'More Catholic than Rome; More Reformed that Geneva: Joseph P. Cassidy and the possibilities for renewal in the Church of England', *International Journal for the Study of the Christian Church* 19.1 (2019), pp. 59–71.